Ephesians
FOR BEGINNERS

MIKE MAZZALONGO

THE "FOR BEGINNERS" SERIES

The "For Beginners" series of video classes and books provide a non-technical and easy to understand presentation of Bible books and topics that are rich in information and application for the beginner as well as the mature Bible student.

bibletalk.tv/for-beginners

Copyright © 2015 by Mike Mazzalongo

ISBN: 978-0692454015

BibleTalk Books
14998 E. Reno
Choctaw, Oklahoma 73020

Scripture quotations taken from the New American Standard Bible®, Copyright © 1960, 1962, 1963, 1968, 1971, 1972, 1973, 1975, 1977, 1995 by The Lockman Foundation Used by permission. (www.Lockman.org)

TABLE OF CONTENTS

1. INTRODUCTION TO EPHESIANS	7
2. THE CITY AND CHURCH OF EPHESUS	17
3. ALL SPIRITUAL BLESSINGS IN CHRIST	27
4. PAST – PRESENT – FUTURE OF THE CHURCH	35
5. THE BASICS FOR UNITY IN THE CHURCH	43
6. GOD'S BLESSING TO THE GENTILES	51
7. UNITY OF THE CHURCH	59
8. THE RESPONSE OF RIGHTEOUSNESS	67
9. TRUE PIETY	73
10. AN ORDERED LIFE	79
11. FAITHFULNESS	87

INTRODUCTION

Ephesians has been called the queen of the epistles because of the lofty ideas contained in its opening chapter, and also because it focuses on the spiritual nature of the church.

The "for beginners" approach of this book will help readers become familiar with Paul's teachings in this letter and gain for them a greater appreciation for the church itself and its centrality in God's purpose for man.

1.
INTRODUCTION TO EPHESIANS

The Ephesian letter has been called the queen of the epistles because of the very lofty ideas contained in chapter one, and because it deals with the church as a spiritual rather than a physical entity.

The objectives of this book examining Paul's letter to this church are that:

- The reader becomes familiar with the teachings contained in the Ephesian letter.

- The reader gains a greater appreciation for the church and its centrality in God's purpose for man.

- The reader becomes sensitized to the great difference between the physical realm and the spiritual realm in which we live simultaneously as Christians.

By the end of our study, I hope that everyone who reads this book will have a clearer view of God, His church and the very real blessings/powers we possess as Christians.

Paul's Ministry – 32 AD to 67 AD

We know that Paul is the author of the epistle, and wrote it as a result of his visits there. Before we actually begin the text, I thought it would be helpful if we briefly reviewed Paul's ministry since much of it is interwoven with the work he did in Ephesus.

Birth to 31 AD

Paul's early life in Tarsus and Jerusalem

Paul was born in the city of Tarsus and as a citizen of this city was granted automatic Roman citizenship (Philippians 3:5). He traced his lineage to the Jewish tribe of Benjamin (Acts 16:37).

Tarsus was a city of learning and this is where Paul became acquainted with Greek learning and language as well as various religious cults. He received his formal education at the feet of Gamaliel (the great Jewish teacher) in Jerusalem (Acts 7:58; Galatians 1:13).

As a young man he was given authority to direct the persecution of Christians, and as a member of the local synagogue or Sanhedrin (council) he cast his vote against Christians in order to imprison or execute them (Acts 26:10). We think that his family was of some prominence in Jerusalem since we see that when he himself was imprisoned he sent his nephew directly to the Roman leaders to inform them of a plot by the Jews to kill him. This could not have happened without a position of influence (Acts 23:16-20).

We have little information about Paul's early years other than he was probably a widower since he encouraged the unmarried (widows/widowers/divorced) at Corinth to remain as he was, unmarried (I Corinthians 7:8), for the sake of peace in times of persecution. We believe he was a widower because he refers to himself as such, and one had to be married to be on the council in the synagogue or Sanhedrin.

We know very little of his looks. I Corinthians 2:3 and II Corinthians 10:10 suggest that his physical appearance was not impressive. Some non-biblical but historical writings (The Acts of Paul and Thella) say that he was short and balding, had crooked legs but a healthy body and bushy eyebrows that joined along with a hooked nose. They also write that despite his humble physical appearance, he was full of grace and sometimes had the face of an angel.

32 AD to 34 AD
Conversion and early ministry

Of course, most of our knowledge of him begins with his conversion on the road to Damascus. He had received official orders to go there and arrest Christians (Acts 9:1-2). He was acquainted with Christianity and Christians but as a persecutor of the church. The Bible records his participation in two such persecutions:

- Stephen - Acts 7:54-60
- The church - Acts 8:1-ff

On his way to Damascus, in order to carry out attacks against Christians in that city, Paul had an encounter with Jesus Christ that left him without sight (Acts 9:3-9). He fasted and prayed for three days until a Christian named Ananias was sent to him by the Lord to heal him of his blindness. Ananias also preached the Gospel to Paul and revealed to him the nature of his future ministry, which we know would be to preach the Gospel to the Gentiles (Acts 9:10-18).

After his healing and conversion, he began his ministry by preaching to the Jews in Damascus. He was quite successful at this (Acts 9:20-22). During this period he also spent time in the desert devoting himself to prayer and study (Galatians 1:17). Eventually he had to escape from

Damascus because of the pressure from the Jews (Acts 9:23-25).

35 AD
Tries to associate with Apostles

After his escape from Damascus he returns to Jerusalem and tries to associate with the Apostles and be recognized by them (Acts 9:26). They were skeptical at first but with Barnabas' reference and commendation of his conversion and work, he was accepted by the Apostles and began to teach and preach there. Again he was threatened and had to escape (Acts 9:27-30).

36 AD to 42 AD
Return to Tarsus

After Paul left Jerusalem he returned to his hometown of Tarsus and spent several years preaching and teaching there (Acts 9:30). Some scholars call this his "silent period."

42 AD to 44 AD
Teaches at Antioch

The church at Antioch was the first to have a mixture of Jewish and non-Jewish Christians, having been formed as Christians escaped persecution in Jerusalem. This created a severe "strain" on the fellowship there and so Barnabas recruited Paul to come with him to teach and preach at this place (Acts 11:19-26).

44 AD
Helps with "collection" for Jerusalem

About this time Jerusalem, with the surrounding area, suffered famine conditions. A collection was taken to help out, and Barnabas and Saul were put in charge of bringing it to Jerusalem for distribution (Acts 11:27-30).

45 AD to 57 AD
Missionary journeys

Most of the last half of the book of Acts describes Paul's three missionary journeys (Acts 13). It is during the second of these journeys that he first visits the city of Ephesus where he will eventually establish a congregation (Acts 18:18-21). I will provide more details about this in the next chapter.

His three journeys took him on ever widening loops around the Mediterranean area where he would establish churches on the way out, and revisit and strengthen them on his return to Antioch or Jerusalem.

58 AD to 60 AD
Prison at Caesarea

One of Paul's ongoing problems was the attack of Jewish leaders jealous of his success, and fear that their religion would be defiled or displaced. On one of his returns to Jerusalem, the Jewish leaders created a riot and caused him to be imprisoned by Roman authorities. He remained in a Roman jail for two years while local rulers like Felix, Festus and Agrippa held him captive to appease local Jewish leaders (Acts 21:15-26:30). Ultimately, Paul appealed his case to Caesar, which he was allowed to do as a Roman citizen, and was sent to Rome for trial.

60 AD to 61 AD
Trip to Rome

The trip by ship to Rome was interrupted by a shipwreck and stay on the island of Malta. Eventually in the spring of 61 AD Paul arrived in Rome (Acts 28:11).

His arrival in Rome was ironic because one of Paul's goals was to preach in the Empire's capital city, and now he found himself there not as a preacher but as a prisoner.

61 AD to 63 AD
Roman house arrest

Luke tells us (Acts 28:30) that Paul was under a type of house arrest for two years awaiting trial. However, during this time he taught many who visited him (eventually the Jewish leaders in Rome rejected him, Acts 28:29). He did, however, have great success with many Gentiles in Rome, including the other prisoners and guards in his circle (Onesimus, Colossians 4:9; Praetorian Guard, Philippians 1:13). While in prison he wrote several letters to different churches (prison epistles). We have four of these remaining: Ephesians, Philippians, Colossians and Philemon.

63 AD
Release from prison

It seems that Paul won his case when he appeared before Caesar the first time because we see him visiting other churches after his arrest and imprisonment in Rome.

64 AD to 66 AD
Revisits churches

This period is less clear than his previous activity. There is no biblical evidence, but there are some historical writings (Letter of Clement, 95 AD) that say that he did visit Spain after his first Roman imprisonment.

From his writings, however, we do find out that during this time he revisited established congregations.

- He spent time in Crete (a large island in the Mediterranean) – Titus 1:3
- He went to Ephesus – I Timothy 1:3
- He travelled to Corinth – II Timothy 4:20
- He stopped at Troas – II Timothy 4:13
- He went to Miletus – II Timothy 4:20

During this brief period of freedom it is believed that he wrote the first letter to Timothy and the letter to Titus.

67 AD
Paul martyred in Rome

In 64 AD Nero burned down the city of Rome and to divert blame from himself, he blamed Christians for starting the blaze. They were already unpopular and so it was easy to begin this persecution. Multitudes of Roman Christians were arrested and put to death during this time. Paul, as a recognized leader, was rearrested during this period. It is from his cell, awaiting execution, that he writes his final letter to Timothy (II Timothy). He was beheaded soon after. This ended the life of one of the great servants of the Lord.

Paul and Ephesus

Paul's Missionary Journeys – 45 to 57 AD

Acts 18:18-21 – Paul was on his second missionary journey on his way home from Athens, Greece. He visits briefly to an enthusiastic response and leaves Aquila and Priscilla there in order to return home to report on his work. There were no conversions at this time.

Acts 18:24-28 – Apollos comes to Ephesus and preaches to the same people that Paul did. We find the results of his preaching in the next chapter, but Luke writes that Paul's friends, Aquila and Priscilla, take Apollos aside and teach him more accurately "…the way of God." Again, only in the next chapter do we get some idea of what Apollos was taught by them.

Acts 19:1-7 – Paul returns for a second visit to Ephesus and establishes the church. He finds twelve believers who have been taught exclusively by Apollos. Paul learns that they have been incorrectly taught by asking about their conversions.

Part of the basic Christian Gospel is that through Christ and His baptism the Holy Spirit is received (Acts 2:38). Their answer shows that what Apollos taught them was the message of John the Baptist. John's message was to repent and be baptized in preparation for the Kingdom that was coming. This is what Apollos taught them.

The message of the Gospel is that the Kingdom of God has come with power and those who repent and are baptized in Jesus' name are forgiven and receive the Holy Spirit. It is the Holy Spirit that is the power of the Kingdom because He empowers us to minister and to resurrect from the dead (Romans 8:9-11).

To the Jews, the fact that the Holy Spirit was given through Christ was the big issue about the Gospel, what they had been promised by prophets (i.e. Joel). This is what Paul teaches their men and what Aquila and Priscilla taught Apollos after they heard him speak.

Note that the disciples are re-baptized. Have you ever wondered why? They were first baptized the right way (immersion) but for the wrong reasons (John the Baptist's promise of the Kingdom).

Question - Why wasn't Apollos re-baptized?

Answer - All the ones baptized by John the Baptist when he was preaching were not re-baptized when Christ's baptism was begun on Pentecost. This is because John's baptism fulfilled all righteousness at the time it was preached. There was, therefore, no need to re-baptize people who received John's baptism from John himself or his disciples at the time of John the Baptist's ministry. Apollos was one of these, as were the Apostles.

Once Peter preached at Pentecost, however, only Christ's baptism was valid and every one still receiving John's baptism needed to be re-baptized. And so, with the re-baptism of these twelve men by Paul, the church at Ephesus was established.

For a more complete discussion concerning the issue of re-baptism, see "Appendix A" at the back of this book.

2. THE CITY AND CHURCH OF EPHESUS

Here is what we've learned so far about the Ephesian letter:

- Paul, on his second missionary journey returning from Athens in Greece, stops for a short time to teach in the city of Ephesus.

- He leaves, promising to return in the future.

- When he returns, he re-baptizes some men (12) who had been taught by Apollos and with these twelve the church in Ephesus is established.

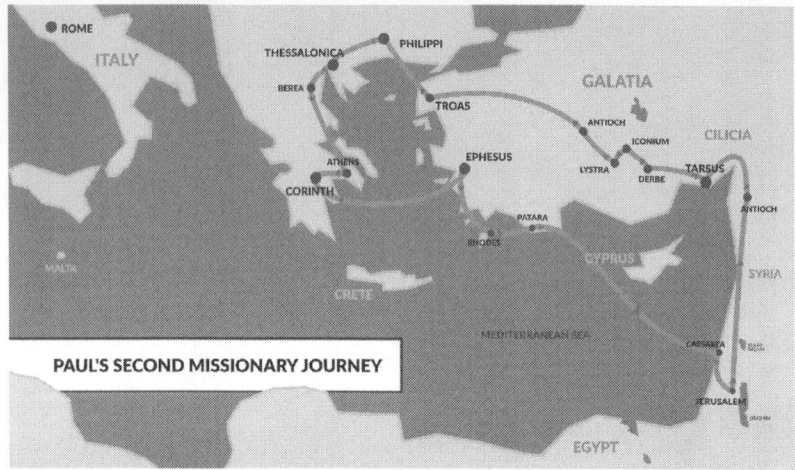

In this chapter we will look at the city of Ephesus itself as well as Paul's early work there, and then begin a study of his letter to these brethren. The story of the beginning of this church is found in Acts 19.

Background: Ephesus, the City

Ephesus itself was a great city for that time.

- It was situated in modern day Turkey.
- It served as a major port for Asia Minor.
- There was a street 70' wide that ran from the port through the entire city.
- The population at that time was approximately 300,000 people.
- Many streets were lined with marble and had public baths and a theatre that held between 25,000 and 50,000 people.
- The temple to the goddess Diana, regarded as one of the 7 wonders of the ancient world (100 pillars held the roof) was situated there.

- Diana was a fertility goddess and drew pilgrims from all over the world.
- Around the temple was a community that housed artisans who made a good living making coins, statues, etc. They had a guild/union.
- In Ephesus the culture, religion and politics were mixed together as one entity.

[8] And he entered the synagogue and continued speaking out boldly for three months, reasoning and persuading them about the kingdom of God. [9] But when some were becoming hardened and disobedient, speaking evil of the Way before the people, he withdrew from them and took away the disciples, reasoning daily in the school of Tyrannus. [10] This took place for two years, so that all who lived in Asia heard the word of the Lord, both Jews and Greeks.

[11] God was performing extraordinary miracles by the hands of Paul, [12] so that handkerchiefs or aprons were even carried from his body to the sick, and the diseases left them and the evil spirits went out. [13] But also some of the Jewish exorcists, who went from place to place, attempted to name over those who had the evil spirits the name of the Lord Jesus, saying, "I adjure you by Jesus whom Paul preaches." [14] Seven sons of one Sceva, a Jewish chief priest, were doing this. [15] And the evil spirit answered and said to them, "I recognize Jesus, and I know about Paul, but who are you?" [16] And the man, in whom was the evil spirit, leaped on them and subdued all of them and overpowered them, so that they fled out of that house naked and wounded. [17] This became known to all, both Jews and Greeks, who lived in Ephesus; and fear fell

> upon them all and the name of the Lord Jesus was being magnified. [18] Many also of those who had believed kept coming, confessing and disclosing their practices. [19] And many of those who practiced magic brought their books together and began burning them in the sight of everyone; and they counted up the price of them and found it fifty thousand pieces of silver. [20] So the word of the Lord was growing mightily and prevailing.
> - Acts 19:8-20

Note that the growth of the church was not only confined to the city of Ephesus, but Christians from Ephesus evangelized the entire region.

The riot

> [21] Now after these things were finished, Paul purposed in the Spirit to go to Jerusalem after he had passed through Macedonia and Achaia, saying, "After I have been there, I must also see Rome." [22] And having sent into Macedonia two of those who ministered to him, Timothy and Erastus, he himself stayed in Asia for a while.
> - Acts 19:21-22

Paul feels that the church is well established so he sends two workers ahead of him to prepare for his next trip to northern Greece and Rome, and then returning home to Jerusalem. After sending his men ahead he remained a little while longer to strengthen the church in Ephesus. This is when trouble happens.

> [23] About that time there occurred no small disturbance concerning the Way. [24] For a man named Demetrius, a silversmith, who made silver shrines of Artemis, was bringing no little business to the craftsmen; [25] these he gathered together with the workmen of similar trades, and said,

"Men, you know that our prosperity depends upon this business. ²⁶ You see and hear that not only in Ephesus, but in almost all of Asia, this Paul has persuaded and turned away a considerable number of people, saying that gods made with hands are no gods at all. ²⁷ Not only is there danger that this trade of ours fall into disrepute, but also that the temple of the great goddess Artemis be regarded as worthless and that she whom all of Asia and the world worship will even be dethroned from her magnificence."

²⁸ When they heard this and were filled with rage, they began crying out, saying, "Great is Artemis of the Ephesians!" ²⁹ The city was filled with the confusion, and they rushed with one accord into the theater, dragging along Gaius and Aristarchus, Paul's traveling companions from Macedonia. ³⁰ And when Paul wanted to go into the assembly, the disciples would not let him. ³¹ Also some of the Asiarchs who were friends of his sent to him and repeatedly urged him not to venture into the theater. ³² So then, some were shouting one thing and some another, for the assembly was in confusion and the majority did not know for what reason they had come together. ³³ Some of the crowd concluded it was Alexander, since the Jews had put him forward; and having motioned with his hand, Alexander was intending to make a defense to the assembly. ³⁴ But when they recognized that he was a Jew, a single outcry arose from them all as they shouted for about two hours, "Great is Artemis of the Ephesians!" ³⁵ After quieting the crowd, the town clerk said, "Men of Ephesus, what man is there after all who does not know that the city of the Ephesians is guardian of the temple of the great Artemis and of the image which fell down from heaven? ³⁶ So, since these are undeniable facts, you ought to keep calm and to do nothing rash. ³⁷ For you have brought these men here who are neither robbers of temples nor

> blasphemers of our goddess. ³⁸ So then, if Demetrius and the craftsmen who are with him have a complaint against any man, the courts are in session and proconsuls are available; let them bring charges against one another. ³⁹ But if you want anything beyond this, it shall be settled in the lawful assembly. ⁴⁰ For indeed we are in danger of being accused of a riot in connection with today's events, since there is no real cause for it, and in this connection we will be unable to account for this disorderly gathering." ⁴¹ After saying this he dismissed the assembly. - Acts 19:23-41

The preaching of the gospel had begun to threaten the business surrounding Diana worship so the local businessmen stirred up a riot accusing Paul and his companions of civil disruption and disrespect for the local deity.

- Artemis is the Greek word for Diana (Latin).
- Diana was said to have fallen from the sky. In reality, it was a meteorite that fell and was eventually encased in the entrance to the temple.
- Artemis was the sister of Apollo, daughter of Jupiter and Latona in Greek mythology.

Eventually one of the city leaders quelled the riot by pointing out that they were breaking Roman law by doing this. The riot and the threatened execution of a Roman citizen (Paul) was unlawful since Rome controlled this territory. The problem that Paul was having in Ephesus was that Christianity refused any form of syncretism (the mixture together of religions). Pagan religions were often a mixture of several belief systems; Hinduism, for example, is like this. This is why many Hindus accept Christ and simply add Him to their Hindu belief system.

A feature of true biblical Christianity is that it refuses to be mixed into any other religion and does not include the non-biblical principles of other religions into its theology, but it does adapt itself to every culture and generation (like the Church of Christ in China, Africa, etc.).

It was this refusal to allow pagan Diana worship to influence the Christian faith, and the demand that idol worshippers abandon this practice that caused all the trouble for those who were preaching Christ and His exclusive demands on His followers.

The Letter: Time / Author

After Paul left Ephesus he went north to Greece and ultimately made his way back home to Jerusalem with a final stop on the island of Miletus (an island near the coast where the city of Ephesus was located). He did this because he wanted to avoid any problems or delays in his travel plans that might arise if he stopped in Ephesus itself (Acts 20:1-38). While there he called for the elders from Ephesus to meet with him and gave them important instructions concerning their work. They, in turn, bid him a tearful farewell.

Once he returns to Jerusalem, we learn from the final chapters of Acts that Paul is imprisoned for a long period of time and ultimately goes to Rome to stand trial before Caesar.

While Paul is under house arrest in Rome (61-63 AD) he is visited by a succession of preachers and messengers from various congregations giving him various reports on the condition and progress of different congregations Paul had established or had worked with. For example, people like Epaphroditus, Timothy and Tychicus were all sent back with letters Paul had written to encourage and teach their different churches.

We have copies of four of these letters written by Paul while in Rome. He may have written more and there is evidence that he did, but four remain: Ephesians, Philippians, Colossians and Philemon.

Three of these four were written at the same time and sent by one messenger. Onesimus, a runaway slave, was converted by Paul in prison and returned to his master, Philemon, with a letter. Philemon was a member at Colossae so the letter for that church was also brought by Onesimus. Ephesus was 100 miles west of Colossae so Onesimus dropped it off on his way home. The fourth letter, to the Philippians, was delivered by Epaphroditus.

There is little doubt that Paul is the author of the letter to the Ephesians in that he names himself in the first verse, and many historical writings show that Paul was universally credited by the early church as being the author of these four epistles. In other words, this is an authentic letter from the Apostle Paul, and was recognized as such from the very beginning.

Reasons for the letter

There were many problems being faced by the 1st century church as it sought to be established and grow in a pagan society. There were the immoral influences of pagan society within the Roman Empire of that period as well as the open and active persecution of the church.

There were also the dangers of false teachers creeping into the church with uninspired teachings. For example, many teachers of that time mixed Greek philosophical thought with Christianity, or mixed Jewish law-keeping and ceremonial law with the gospel of grace, and then there was the danger of syncretism with pagan religions that were common in that time and place.

There was also the problem of getting Jewish and Gentile converts to live together in harmony as brothers and sisters in Christ. These people came from wildly different cultures and religious practices.

Most of Paul's letters deal with difficult issues: immorality and proper conduct (I Corinthians), mixing of the Greek and Jewish ideas with the gospel of Christ (Colossians), an appeal to Jewish Christians to accept their Gentile brethren in Christ (Galatians). In Ephesians Paul makes an appeal to Gentile Christians not to exclude Jewish Christians (or anyone else for that matter) from inclusion in the church. It was an appeal to those (Gentiles) who had no sentimental, cultural or historical ties to the Jewish religion. Paul encourages them to be tolerant and accepting of those whose history and relationship to a Jewish messiah was still very important!

Paul did not want to see two churches: one Jewish, one Gentile. He wanted both of these to be accommodated in one body and one body only. His defense of the Gentiles was seen in his teaching and associating with them while calling out to his Jewish brethren to accept them as full partners in Christ. His appeal (from Gentiles to Jesus) was seen in his effort to collect money from Gentile churches in order to help the Jews in Jerusalem suffering from a crippling famine (I Corinthians 16). If Christian Jews had problems accepting Gentile Christians, this gift was meant to break down resistance and suspicion.

In his letter to Ephesians (who were experiencing divisiveness between Jews and Gentiles), Paul describes a church that is big enough and loving enough to include Jewish and Gentile Christians, as well as people of different genders, viewpoints and experiences. In addition to this, Paul demonstrates in this epistle how unity and order in the church, the family, in society and in the spiritual world can be achieved through Jesus Christ, who is the head of the body of believers. It is interesting to note that Ephesians is the only letter where Paul uses the word "church" in the "universal" and not in the local congregational sense.

One commentator has called Ephesians the epistle of the church. The book of Acts describes the physical history of the church. The book of Ephesians describes its character.

Outline: Ephesians

1. Blessings of the church – 1:1-23
2. Universality of the church – 2:1-3:21
3. Obligations of the church
    a. Unity – 4:1-16
    b. Righteousness – 4:17-6:9
    c. Faithfulness – 6:10-24

Ephesians, more than any other epistle, demonstrates how important and how central the church is to God's plan and His purpose for mankind.

3.
ALL SPIRITUAL BLESSINGS IN CHRIST

EPHESIANS 1:1-23

We reviewed the fact that the Ephesian letter was written by Paul while he was imprisoned in Rome between 61-63 AD. It was delivered to Ephesus by Onesimus, a slave returning to his master in Colossae, located about 100 miles west of Ephesus. This man had been converted in prison and sent back by Paul with several letters to deliver, among them this one to the Ephesians. Ephesus was a key congregation in an important location and much of the evangelization of the area was begun from this point. Ephesus flourished as a church, but in time began to lag in its original zeal, so a warning was given to it by John the Apostle in the book of Revelation some 30 years later. After Paul left Ephesus, John came to work and settle there until his last days. The book of Ephesians can be divided in several ways, and I have already provided one possible outline:

1. Blessings of the church – 1:1-23
2. Universality of the church – 2:1-3:21
3. Obligations of the church
    a. Unity – 4:1-16
    b. Righteousness – 4:17-6:9
    c. Faithfulness – 6:10-24

The thing to remember about Ephesians, however, is that it is a letter that focuses on the importance of the church in God's plan. In his letter, Paul says four main things about the church:

1. That the creation and blessing of the church was the objective that God had from the beginning of time.

2. That true "living" can only be experienced as a member of the body of Christ and that everyone could be part of that body (church).

3. That the church is the "light" in society as far as setting the standard for what is right, how to treat one another and the revelation of Christ in His Word.

4. That in the end the church will arise as victorious over every physical and spiritual entity, including death.

So, keeping all of this in mind, let us go into the first chapter and examine the blessings that Paul says are reserved only for the church.

The Blessings

The first chapter and section are divided into two parts.

1. The Greetings

> [1] Paul, an apostle of Christ Jesus by the will of God, To the saints who are at Ephesus and who are faithful in Christ Jesus: [2] Grace to you and peace from God our Father and the Lord Jesus Christ.

As was the custom, Paul introduces himself at the beginning of the letter. Note that he also establishes his own credibility and authority as an inspired Apostle, not self-appointed but appointed by God. He also recognizes them as faithful saints; not every church was so addressed since some congregations had problems and the letters sent to them were letters of rebuke (Corinthians). Again, he completes his greetings with a familiar blessing: "Grace to you and peace from God our Father and the Lord Jesus Christ." Grace was that quality of God that led Him to offer salvation through the death of His Son (instead of universal condemnation). Peace was the result of that gracious action on God's part. There would now be peace between all men who believed in Jesus and God. There would also be peace in every saved person's soul.

This was a way that Paul compressed the entire gospel message and its effect on mankind in just a few words, and offer it as a blessing to those who knew the details and significance behind these words.

2. God's Purpose

> [3] Blessed be the God and Father of our Lord Jesus Christ, who has blessed us with every spiritual blessing in the heavenly places in Christ, [4] just as He chose us in Him before the foundation of the world, that we would be holy and blameless before Him. In love [5] He predestined us to adoption as sons through Jesus Christ to Himself, according to the kind intention

> of His will, [6] to the praise of the glory of His grace, which He freely bestowed on us in the Beloved. [7] In Him we have redemption through His blood, the forgiveness of our trespasses, according to the riches of His grace [8] which He lavished on us. In all wisdom and insight [9] He made known to us the mystery of His will, according to His kind intention which He purposed in Him [10] with a view to an administration suitable to the fullness of the times, that is, the summing up of all things in Christ, things in the heavens and things on the earth. In Him [11] also we have obtained an inheritance, having been predestined according to His purpose who works all things after the counsel of His will, [12] to the end that we who were the first to hope in Christ would be to the praise of His glory. [13] In Him, you also, after listening to the message of truth, the gospel of your salvation—having also believed, you were sealed in Him with the Holy Spirit of promise, [14] who is given as a pledge of our inheritance, with a view to the redemption of God's own possession, to the praise of His glory.

In the second part of this section Paul will discuss God's essential purpose when it comes to the church. God's purpose from the beginning of time was to create an entity (church / body of Christ / Christians / saints / the saved / the redeemed etc.) upon whom He could lavish spiritual blessings. The Bible is the account of how He accomplished this; Jesus Christ is the person through whom He accomplished this; the church is that "thing" (entity) He did it for. In verses 3-14 Paul describes the nature of the blessings (gifts) that God gives to the church through Jesus Christ.

Vs. 3 – God blesses, or gives gifts that are spiritual in nature, to the church in connection with Jesus. God has given to believers all of the available gifts. These gifts are given and received because of and in relation to Jesus Christ only! "In Christ" is the term that Paul uses to express this idea.

Election – The idea of election is that God chooses (elects) Jesus Christ and those who are united to Him by faith, to be the ones who receive the blessings. Election does not refer to some process where God arbitrarily chooses who is to be saved and who is to be lost.

Vs. 4a – The decision to choose Christ as the Savior and save those who believe in Him was made before the beginning of time, and not an afterthought. All of history fits into this plan. Paul describes some of the blessings that God has prepared to give to the church:

Vs. 4b – Those in Christ would be holy and blameless, without impurity. They would have no imperfections, be without condemnation and able to look at God without fear.

Vs. 5-6 – Those in Christ become sons of God and recipients of His grace.

Vs. 7-8 – Those in Christ have forgiveness because their sins have been redeemed (moral debt has been paid for by Christ's death).

Vs. 9-10 – Those in Christ have insight into God's overall plan for man, which is not stated fully here in this passage. However Paul explains a little further on that God's plan is to unite all the saved (Jew and Greek), to separate the saved from the unsaved at judgment, and then to unite the saved with the Godhead forever.

Vs. 11-12 – Those in Christ become God's witnesses here on earth (salvation and light). The church is the vehicle by which God is revealed and through which God is praised. The church is here to provide praise and provoke praise to God from others. By virtue of its very existence, the church is praise to God.

Vs. 13-14 – Those in Christ have possession of God's Holy Spirit as a gift for their own spiritual pleasure (it is delightful to commune with God intimately). In addition, the possession of the Spirit is the identifying factor that guarantees the other promises (resurrection, eternal life, etc.). God gives these to those who have the Holy Spirit and He knows who these are.

These are the major gifts that those who are united to Jesus by faith (expressed in repentance and baptism) and referred to as being "in Christ" possess.

The Value of the Gifts "in Christ"

> [15] For this reason I too, having heard of the faith in the Lord Jesus which exists among you and your love for all the saints, [16] do not cease giving thanks for you, while making mention of you in my prayers; [17] that the God of our Lord Jesus Christ, the Father of glory, may give to you a spirit of wisdom and of revelation in the knowledge of Him. [18] I pray that the eyes of your heart may be enlightened, so that you will know what is the hope of His calling, what are the riches of the glory of His inheritance in the saints, [19] and what is the surpassing greatness of His power toward us who believe. These are in accordance with the working of the strength of His might [20] which He brought about in Christ, when He raised Him from the dead and seated Him at His right hand in the heavenly places, [21] far above all rule and authority and power and dominion, and every name that is named, not only in this age but also in the one to come. [22] And He put all things in subjection under His feet, and gave Him as head over all things to the church, [23] which is His body, the fullness of Him who fills all in all.

After receiving the blessings that God bestows on those who are in Christ, Paul expresses a prayer in which he asks God to help his readers understand more deeply the nature and value of the gifts they possess. Like the gift of youth that many older people say is wasted on the young, these are young Christians and so Paul wants them to appreciate what they have and not squander it.

Prayer for the church

Vs. 15-17 – Because they have been faithful as a young church, despite persecution, Paul prays that God will give them the ability to know God more intimately. Heaven will be the experience of having a relationship with God without the hindrance of sin and death. He wants them to begin experiencing this phenomena now.

Vs. 18-19 – In this passage he describes in more detail some of the things he wants them to know about God that will prove to be a blessing to them. He wants them to know: the hope before them (vs. 18a), the riches of the inheritance (vs. 18b), and the greatness of His power (vs. 19). All refer to the same thing: our resurrection, glorification and exaltation to reign with God forever. He wants them to be able to see what wonderful things these will be.

Vs. 20-23 – In these verses Paul completes his prayer by describing how these blessings were acquired and how they are presently administered. Those in Christ will be resurrected and be with God in heaven because that's where Jesus is now. He prays that they can appreciate more and more the rewards that they have been called to receive as disciples of Jesus, who guarantees them by virtue of His sovereignty over all things.

Summary

Here are several things we can learn from this passage:

1. Spiritual blessings are only available if one is united with Christ through faith. We need to verify if we have faith and if it has been expressed as Jesus would have it (repentance and baptism).

2. Spiritual blessings are far more valuable than material ones, yet they are given for free. If we were

truly spiritual we would worry less about trying to gain and keep material things and spend a little more time in search of the spiritual and eternal blessings. After all, Jesus said, "What will a man give in exchange for his soul?"

3. Spiritual blessings are appreciated and enhanced through the activity of prayer. Paul prayed for them to begin experiencing the joy associated with the blessings they had. Many times what's missing in our spiritual lives is prayer or prayer to know God and appreciate His gifts more. When we literally have everything but are not enjoying it, usually this is because we don't understand that spiritual things are tasted, contemplated, and experienced in the dimension of prayer, service, worship, sacrifice and obedience. The first step to heaven usually begins by getting on our knees.

4.
PAST – PRESENT – FUTURE OF THE CHURCH

EPHESIANS 2:1-10

Let's review what we have learned so far in our study of Paul's letter to the Ephesian church:

1. Paul greets and compliments them on their faithfulness.
2. He explains to them that God's purpose, from before the beginning of time, was to create and bless the church with all the blessings that exist in heaven.
3. He goes on to name and describe these spiritual gifts:

    - Purity and innocence bestowed, not earned
    - Adoption as children of God
    - Forgiveness of sin

- Insight into God's plan: to save them and unite them to Himself
- The ability of the church to be given as an offering of praise to God
- Possession of the Holy Spirit
- Assurance of resurrection, glorification, and exaltation

4. He continues his prayer to include the request that God "enable" them to know Him more intimately; see more clearly the assurance or hope that they've been given; recognize the source from which comes all of these blessings; and perceive the glorious end that Christ and His church were to experience (resurrection, glorification, exaltation).

I also mentioned that these blessings are only available if one is united to Christ through faith (expressed in repentance and baptism) and are appreciated and enhanced through prayer. In the first chapter of this epistle Paul describes the blessings that God has prepared for the church through Christ. In chapters two and three he will describe the universal nature of the church.

In the last verse of chapter one Paul refers to Christ as the head of all things (something he explains more in detail in the letter to the Colossians 1:15-ff). In that letter he describes Christ as the One who is head over creation, head over the spiritual world as well as head over the church. In Ephesians he summarizes this idea by referring to Christ's rule in heaven, rule over all things, and leadership over the church (1:22). Very much like Colossians, this imagery of Christ as "head" over the body (the church) is used as a bridge to transfer from one set of ideas (prayer for their blessings) to another set of ideas (nature of the church). So we leave the discussion about the blessings, and move on to a broader teaching about the church "in time," which will become the overall theme of this letter.

The Past

> ¹ And you were dead in your trespasses and sins, ² in which you formerly walked according to the course of this world, according to the prince of the power of the air, of the spirit that is now working in the sons of disobedience. ³ Among them we too all formerly lived in the lusts of our flesh, indulging the desires of the flesh and of the mind, and were by nature children of wrath, even as the rest.

Paul begins by describing the past condition of every member of the church before they became part of the body of Christ.

Vs. 1 – The word "dead" means "…to be separated" from God. For example, a branch cut from a tree seems alive but is really dead because it has been cut away from the source of its life which is the tree.

Vs. 2 – The Apostle explains that they were dead (separated) because their lives were governed by three principles:

1. The course of the world: people separated from God live according to the principles of *this* world. The problem here is that worldly principles cannot regenerate man's spiritual life with God (i.e., give life to that cut off branch).

2. The Prince and Power of the Air: people will serve one of two authorities. Those separated from God end up serving Satan whether they realize it or not, and his goal is to keep us away from Christ.

3. The Spirit of the Sons of Disobedience: people separated from God follow the spirit that is within them ("just follow your heart"). This may help you win a

singing contest but it won't save your soul. Man is doomed without God's leadership. *"There is a way which seems right to a man, but its end is the way of death." (Proverbs 14:12)*

Vs. 3 – Paul was speaking of Gentiles, but now includes himself and the Jewish brethren of Ephesus when he describes the outcome of this style of life serving the world, Satan and self. The outcome, Paul says, was that they searched only to satisfy their earthly desires without regard for God (slaves to the flesh), and because of this idolatry, sinfulness and godlessness, they were all subject to the wrath of God's judgment. So Paul summarizes the human condition of unbelievers before they entered the body. This was the shared past of the church.

The Present and the Future

> [4] But God, being rich in mercy, because of His great love with which He loved us, [5] even when we were dead in our transgressions, made us alive together with Christ (by grace you have been saved), [6] and raised us up with Him, and seated us with Him in the heavenly places in Christ Jesus, [7] so that in the ages to come He might show the surpassing riches of His grace in kindness toward us in Christ Jesus.

Vs. 4 – Paul says, "But…" He has described man's hopeless situation and now goes on to say what God has done about it. Let's skip over verse four for the moment and look at verses five and six where Paul explains what God has done in the face of man's actions.

Vs. 5-6 – What God did:

- He made us alive again with Christ. How? Through redemption.

- He raised us from the dead. How? Redemption.
- He set us with Christ in heaven. How? Glory and exaltation.

Vs. 7 – The Apostle looks at what God has done from God's perspective of timelessness and eternity; in God's eyes all that Paul has described is already complete. The faithful in Christ have already received the blessings and sit in heaven with Christ. We live with the restriction of time, and perceive the process as it is being carried out step by step in "time," but God sees everything as already complete and Paul is trying to get his readers to see it from God's view and thus be encouraged.

Now let's go back to verse four where Paul explains why God did this. He explains that God did it (blessed us with every spiritual blessing) because He is rich in mercy, and because He is capable of great sympathy, empathy, tenderness, willingness to forgive and He is the epitome of love. God's mercy (His motivation) and love (how He expresses His mercy) is free towards us. God does this because of who He is, and not because of what we do or will do. God's grace is most evident in the fact that He chooses to have mercy on those who do not deserve it, and arranges for our salvation at great cost to Himself.

Paul's Comment

> ^{8} For by grace you have been saved through faith; and that not of yourselves, it is the gift of God; ^{9} not as a result of works, so that no one may boast. ^{10} For we are His workmanship, created in Christ Jesus for good works, which God prepared beforehand so that we would walk in them.

Once he has completed his summary of the Ephesian church's past (they were lost), present (they are now saved), and future (they will be glorified in heaven), Paul makes a comment concerning what he has just written.

Vs. 8-9 – He says that they have been saved due to an attitude of grace on God's part towards them and through a response of faith on their part. He goes on to explain that this is a gift of God and cannot be earned with good deeds. Many have misunderstood and misused this verse of scripture so let us look carefully at each word in context.

Saved – In one word Paul compresses all of the blessings that he has described so far. To be saved or to receive redemption, resurrection, glorification and exaltation is to say the same thing. Salvation is what we have.

Grace – The reason we have salvation is because God is gracious. Man cannot redeem his own sins, regenerate himself, resurrect his own body, transform himself gloriously or put himself at the right hand of God. God does this with His power because He is merciful. He does it as a favor and freely offers it. This is essentially what grace is. A person cannot earn it, pay for it or produce any of the benefits that grace bestows by his own hand. We cannot produce the blessings of grace but we can, however, receive them as gifts.

Faith – People can receive the gift of salvation solely on the condition set by God, and that condition is salvation received by faith. Let me explain, if a person wins a car in some sort of contest, the dealer may only require that the winner come to the dealership to sign the ownership documents and pick up the vehicle. The car is still free, even if there are conditions to take possession of it. In a similar way, God makes belief the condition upon which the gift of salvation is received and the Bible explains how that belief or faith is to be expressed properly. In Acts 2:38 we see that faith is expressed by repenting of one's sins and being baptized in Jesus' name. Having certain ways that God requires us to express our faith does not mean that our salvation is not free. We do not "earn" our salvation simply by fulfilling God's conditions in receiving it.

And so, Paul says that we obtain what would have been impossible for us to receive (salvation) because God chose to be merciful towards us and offer it on a basis of faith expressed in a way that all could do so: repentance and baptism. Why these particular responses? Because repentance and baptism are the signs that man has understood why he is condemned (sin/repentance) and how he is saved (death, burial, resurrection/baptism).

Again, Paul looks at the situation from God's perspective and says that in addition to creating the church in order to lavish blessings upon it in heaven, He also created good works for it to perform while on earth. Not good works to earn heaven, we already have that, but good works so that God will be witnessed, glorified and visible to non-believers (Matthew 5:16, "Let your light shine before men in such a way that they may see your good works and glorify your father who is in heaven").

In the end, the church is a source of praise for God. This is its present and future function. God loves the church and the church loves others.

5.
THE BASICS FOR UNITY IN THE CHURCH

EPHESIANS 2:11-22

In chapter one of Ephesians Paul reviews God's original plan and purpose for the church, to bless it with every spiritual blessing in heaven. He also reviews for his readers what those blessings are. He then changes the course of his prayer from thanksgiving (for these things) to a request for God to enable the Ephesians to truly grasp and appreciate the eternal glory that awaits them in heaven with Christ. In the last verse he makes a transition or bridge to get to his next topic that will center on the church at Ephesus.

In chapter two he begins to discuss the sinful past of those who are now members of the church and how, because of their slavery to their own desires or the course of this world, they were subject to God's condemnation. This gives him the opportunity to remind them of God's grace and mercy in sending Jesus to die for their sins and offer salvation based on faith. Now, we said that God's grace is seen in two ways: that He chose to offer us salvation in the first place instead of leaving us to perish in our sins, and that He offered it on a basis of faith (and not perfectionism) so that all mankind could be saved. We also spent a little time explaining that in the New Testament, faith was properly expressed by belief in Jesus Christ as the Son of God, repentance of sins and baptism (immersion in water). Now that Paul has summarized how and why the church was formed, he will begin to explain its universal nature and deal with a problem that existed among these brethren.

Universal Nature of the Church

So far, Paul has described how God relates to the church as a single unit: all receive blessings, and all are saved in the same way. From an earthly perspective however, the church struggled with issues of strife and religious division because of the cultural and religious differences in each member's background. The major fault line was between Jewish Christians who had been converted from Judaism, and non-Jewish converts (referred to as Gentiles or Greeks) who had largely come out of various pagan religions. Of course, there were other difficult differences to deal with such as male/female or slave/free divides, but in this particular epistle Paul addresses the problem of unity between Jew and Gentile.

It seems that there were poor relations between Jews (who were a minority but had priority in receiving the gospel) and the Gentiles (who were in the majority but were newer converts). If the church was to be universal, as Jesus and the Apostles taught (as well as the Old Testament prophets), then the breech between Jew and Gentile had to be closed. And so, in chapter 2:11-22, Paul turns his attention to the Gentile Christians at Ephesus and explains what Christ has done specifically for them in order to sharpen their gratitude and strengthen their faith.

Position of the Gentiles Before God

> [11] Therefore remember that formerly you, the Gentiles in the flesh, who are called "Uncircumcision" by the so-called "Circumcision," which is performed in the flesh by human hands — [12] remember that you were at that time separate from Christ, excluded from the commonwealth of Israel, and strangers to the covenants of promise, having no hope and without God in the world.

Vs. 11 – Paul says that the Gentiles were uncircumcised. Circumcision was a sign in the flesh that you were included in the covenant between God and Abraham. God promised Abraham protection, blessings and a Messiah. Circumcision was the sign in your body that you were part of this promise in your generation. The Idea was that every time you bathed, had bodily functions, or had sex with your wife you were reminded of the promise and of who you were. To be "uncircumcised" then meant that you were separated from God and not part of the promise; it was a curse. For the Jews it was a sign of pride, for the Gentiles a reminder of their ultimate rejection. Gentiles should be grateful that, as members of the church, God had removed this barrier between them and Himself.

Vs. 12a – They were excluded from the commonwealth of Israel. The commonwealth of Israel describes not only the Jewish culture but also the body of true believers who were regarded as God's people. Gentiles were not considered true believers; they were idolaters and pagans. But now, as members of the church and regardless of culture, they could be considered true believers.

Vs. 12b – They were strangers to the Covenants of Promise. They had not been promised anything by God (land, blessings, Messiah); only the Jews had been promised these things. As members of the church however, they had escaped condemnation and suffering.

Vs. 12c – They had no hope and no God. Their religion was false, and their gods were helpless to provide any comfort or security. As members of the church, however, God Himself was their protector and savior. In contrast to their blessings in Christ were the various relationships that the Gentiles had with the Jews throughout history. Their relationships are not explained here but were quite evident to Paul's Gentile and Jewish readers. To understand the magnitude of this reconciliation between Jews and Gentiles one had to understand their past relationship in various settings.

Relationship between Jews and Gentiles

Before their respective conversions, the Jews and the Gentiles hated one another. The Jews had nothing to do with Gentiles. They misunderstood the admonitions in the Old Testament concerning their separation from the Gentiles and took this too far. God did not want them to be influenced by pagan behavior, and used the Jews to punish and eliminate the pagans in the Promised Land. However, once established, they were to serve as a light to convert the Gentiles to belief in the true God. The Jews usually reacted in extremes; they either copied the Gentiles and fell into idolatry or despised and rejected them without influencing them for God.

Relationship between Jew and Gentile converts to Judaism

If a Gentile did want to convert to Judaism there were several things he had to do: he had to be circumcised, purified in a water ritual and had to offer an animal sacrifice. There were limits however: a Gentile convert could not mingle with the Jews in the inner court of the Temple, they were relegated to an outer court reserved for them. It was in this outer court that merchants and money changers had set up shop rendering this space unsuitable for proper worship and thus depriving the Gentiles access to legitimate temple worship, and incurring the wrath of Jesus (Matthew 21:12-13).

The major idea in Judaism was that there was a separation between God and Jews as well as Jews and Gentiles. The barrier between God and the Jews was demonstrated in that they could only approach God through the priests and only the High Priest could go into the Holy of Holies (presence of God) once per year on behalf of the people. The barrier between God and non-converted Gentiles was made evident by the fact that they were not allowed to enter any part of the temple under pain of death.

God was pure, holy and unapproachable so that Jews had access only through priests, converts had access only through Jews, and Gentiles had no access at all. So their ideas and ways to relate to each other were well ingrained and still very much in the minds of both Jewish and Gentile converts to Christianity at Ephesus.

If we read between the lines it seems that the Gentile Christians, who had been treated as inferior by the Jews in the past, began to despise their Jewish brothers in Christ now that they were equally accepted in the church. It could also be that the Jewish Christians at Ephesus were having a little problem accepting Gentile Christians as equal partners in God's plan of salvation. And so, in the next verses Paul shows how Christ unifies both Jews and Gentiles in the church before God.

Relationship between Jewish and Gentile converts to Christianity

> [13] But now in Christ Jesus you who formerly were far off have been brought near by the blood of Christ. [14] For He Himself is our peace, who made both groups into one and broke down the barrier of the dividing wall, [15] by abolishing in His

> flesh the enmity, which is the Law of commandments contained in ordinances, so that in Himself He might make the two into one new man, thus establishing peace, [16] and might reconcile them both in one body to God through the cross, by it having put to death the enmity.

Vs. 13 – Paul begins by explaining how God reconciles both Jew and Gentile to Himself: by His cross, Jesus eliminates the barrier of sin that separated the Gentile from God. No need for a Jewish priest or any other mediator; Jesus offers His blood to atone for all sin so the Gentile can come before God through Christ at all times.

Vs. 14-16 – The same is also true for the Jew. The difference is that the revelation of this sacrifice and salvation was given to him earlier through the Law, the sacrificial system and the prophets. Both Jew and Gentile were condemned because of sin. The Jew didn't line up to the Law (sin); the Gentile was ignorant of the Law (sin). So both Jew and Gentile are saved and reconciled to God in the same way. The Jew no longer needs the temple, etc.; The Gentile no longer needs the Jewish religion. Now Jew and Gentile are united to God only through Christ (a common savior).

Jew and Gentile united to each other

> [17] And He came and preached peace to you who were far away, and peace to those who were near; [18] for through Him we both have our access in one Spirit to the Father.

The Law kept Jew and Gentile separate from God (neither could obey it) and separate from each other (Law demanded it). Jesus fulfills all the demands of the Law and thus removes its requirements for both Jew and Gentile. Now both groups are united to God and can be united to each other. Why? Because He who fulfills the Law can make a new law, and Jesus makes a new law that demands unity between Jew and Gentile. Jews and Gentiles couldn't break down the wall that separated them through marriage, dialogue, policies or economics. Jesus is the peace upon which they now can be united. He is the bridge that unites them. Through faith in Christ they enter into a unity with God and share one body with Christ. The meeting point is baptism where the old man is buried and the new is raised, and this is the same for Jews and Gentiles.

Three Images of Unity Between Jew and Gentile

> [19] So then you are no longer strangers and aliens, but you are fellow citizens with the saints, and are of God's household, [20] having been built on the foundation of the apostles and prophets, Christ Jesus Himself being the corner stone, [21] in whom the whole building, being fitted together, is growing into a holy temple in the Lord, [22] in whom you also are being built together into a dwelling of God in the Spirit.

The three images of unity include: the kingdom of saints, where Gentiles have the same rights and privileges as Jews; the household, where all members have the same Father; and the spiritual temple, where Christ is the foundation and each member is a stone and God is the builder. The church is at once all of these because everyone is united in and through Christ.

Paul explains the universal nature of the church by outlining the way that God has brought together the most disparate of groups at that time: Jews and Gentiles. In the next chapter, Paul will continue with this theme by discussing his own role in God's plan of creating a body in which all mankind could be united.

6.
GOD'S BLESSING TO THE GENTILES

EPHESIANS 3:1-21

We are in the second main section of the epistle where Paul is demonstrating the universal nature of the church by explaining how God brings both Jews and Gentiles into one body (the church) through Jesus Christ. He has highlighted this idea by showing the extraordinary lengths God has gone to in order to bring Gentiles into the church. The assumption for the reader is that the story of how the Jews were brought into Christ is well known, having been documented by the Old Testament writers and Apostles. The story of God's effort for the Gentiles is now recounted by Paul to his Ephesian brethren. The reason for this is that there were problems between Gentile and Jewish Christians who were having difficulties accepting each other's place in the church. The Jews were in the minority numerically but first to receive the gospel; the Gentiles were in the numerical majority but were the newer converts and less educated religiously.

Previously, we looked at what Paul said to remind the Gentile Christians what God had done for them through Jesus Christ in order to get them where they were. He was doing this to counter feelings of resentment towards the Jews that may have been poisoning their overall Christian attitude, which should have been one of gratitude. The Gentiles should be grateful to God, not resentful towards Jews. Paul says that before they were in Christ they were apart from God, they didn't belong with the people of God, they had no hope of salvation, and even if they were converted to Judaism, they were still considered second class citizens. But, Paul continues, now that they are in Christ they have direct access to God through Christ, they are equal partners with the Jews in the kingdom of God, the family of God, and in the temple of God (all of these refer to the church in one way or another).

In addition to this, Paul says they now have hope of salvation, unity with all, and value as the people of God. With this said Paul ends his comments regarding what God has done for the Gentiles and offers a prayer of thanksgiving on their behalf. He will begin this prayer of thanks in chapter 3:14, but first he has one other thing he wishes to discuss with them. So we begin chapter three of the Ephesian epistle with Paul giving the details of his own very special ministry among the Gentiles. He has listed the things God has done for them, now he will give them some information about the person God has specifically appointed to reach out to them with the gospel.

Paul's Apostolic Ministry to the Gentiles

> [1] For this reason I, Paul, the prisoner of Christ Jesus for the sake of you Gentiles— [2] if indeed you have heard of the stewardship of God's grace which was given to me for you; [3] that by revelation there was made known to me the mystery, as I wrote before in brief.

Vs. 1 – Paul refers back to the original reason why he is in jail: Jewish leaders had him arrested because of their opposition to his work, especially among the Gentiles. Because of this ministry in Christ's name to the Gentiles he has now spent almost three years in jail.

Vs. 2 – Reviews the idea of his own special ministry. His Apostleship is referred to as "grace" because it was understood that he had originally been a persecutor of the church.

Vs. 3 – His Apostleship to the Gentiles (a mystery) was made known to him at his conversion (Acts 22:21, "Go for I will send you far away to the Gentiles.").

He explains in verses 4-7 what God revealed to him when He called him to this special ministry. A ministry that had as its objective the glad news that Gentiles were also eligible to receive God's grace and blessings. This was not made known before, but now has been revealed through Paul's preaching.

This proved to be a difficult issue in the early church. Paul, the persecutor, was given the gift of revealing to the Gentiles the riches available for them in Christ, riches created and preserved in time by God. Riches that men could not obtain (why it was grace) or even understand (why it was enlightenment) but now revealed and given freely to them by God through Christ.

Why the revelation now? In verse 10, Paul says that the unveiling of God's redemptive work would be done in heaven and on earth. Men did not know, angels did not know (I Peter 1:12). Now men know, angels know, and the church is the instrument of this revelation. We see how God considers the church as a precious thing (pillars and support of the truth - I Timothy 3:15). This mystery, hidden for ages, has come to be known through Jesus Christ who is now our mediator to the Father.

In summary, God had a plan to group together all men into one body of saints reconciled to Himself. He prepared and worked His plan to be fulfilled in Jesus Christ (death, burial and resurrection). He used different men, women and angels to accomplish His plan without them knowing the full extent of it. Now that Christ has completed the work, He is using the body of saints (church) itself to reveal His plan to all men and angels too!

Paul asks his readers not to be discouraged on account of his imprisonment. He's been in prison for years and all his work among the Gentiles seems doomed, their position threatened. They may see things in this way, but Paul reassures them in two important ways. First, He describes how their position has always been in God's plan, and second, he reminds them that God considers them as precious in His sight (Ephesians 3:6-11). His imprisonment is a testimony to how important the work among the Gentiles really is and serves as an ongoing symbol. If they realize these things, they will not lose heart. We shouldn't either when we fail, God wants to save us!

Paul's Intercessory Prayer for the Gentile Christians

> [14] For this reason I bow my knees before the Father, [15] from whom every family in heaven and on earth derives its name, [16] that He would grant you, according to the riches of His glory, to be strengthened with power through His Spirit in the inner man, [17] so that Christ may dwell in your hearts through faith; and that you, being rooted and grounded in love, [18] may be able to comprehend with all the saints what is the breadth and length and height and depth, [19] and to know the love of Christ which surpasses knowledge, that you may be filled up to all the fullness of God.

Vs. 14 – Paul picks up where he left off in verse one. Because of God's provision for all men in this most extraordinary way, Paul is moved to pray. He prays to God the Father, who is the source of all mankind (why all men need to be united in Christ in order to come to the Father). Christ makes it possible for all men, separated from God and one another, to be united one to another, and to their spiritual Father. (This is why Jesus is the answer to the problems of the world!)

What does he ask for? Before, Paul asked that God would enlighten them so they could better grasp the blessings they have in Christ. Now he asks that God "strengthen" them in various ways: strengthen the "inner man" which refers to the heart/mind/spirit; strengthen with spiritual power, not human power/ability; strengthen them according to God's ability and resources; provide strength through the Holy Spirit, not through self-will/practice/physical effort. Of course this brings us to another question which is, "How does the Holy Spirit strengthen the inner man with power?" The Bible describes two ways that this happens.

God's Word (Acts 20:32)

Paul also tells us in II Timothy 3:5-16 that God's word can lead us to salvation, teach, examine and correct our thinking and understanding. Also, it can train us to live righteously in service to God and others. The Holy Spirit is the one who brings us God's word (II Peter 1:20-21).

Indwelling (Acts 2:38)

Peter the Apostle tells us that at baptism we not only receive forgiveness of sins but also the indwelling of the Holy Spirit. Some have taught that this means that the Holy Spirit dwells in us only through His word. The concepts and ideas in the word are in our minds and hearts. However, in Romans 8:11 Paul describes a much more dynamic experience and reality of the Spirit of God within us. I believe the Bible teaches that the Holy Spirit (not just the words) resides in the Christian. I can't explain how God's Spirit co-exists with my spirit in my body, and only know that the Bible says that He does and I believe that. But in Ephesians, Paul says the Spirit strengthens the inner man. The question is, "How does he do this?" I can think of three ways the Bible says that the Spirit does this: He intercedes for us (Romans 8:26); the Spirit enables us to connect with God with confidence in prayer and this confidence strengthens our faith and hope; the Spirit comforts us (Acts 9:31). Not the comfort that comes from counseling and encouragement given to us from others that we understand and appreciate, the Holy Spirit's direct comfort that grants us the peace of mind and heart beyond human understanding (everything in my life is falling apart, and yet, I have no fear because the Lord is with me, this kind of comfort).

Enlightenment (Ephesians 1:18)

It's the Holy Spirit that gives this word of enlightening us to God's will and purpose. So Paul prays for God to strengthen the Gentiles in all of these different ways so they can achieve certain spiritual goals. He's prayed for the means to reach the following two ends.

1. To permit them to surrender more of themselves to Christ. Christians need to be strengthened in the inner man, in faith so that Christ can take greater possession of them (i.e. only the spiritually strong can be meek as Christ is meek. Only the spiritually strong can crucify the flesh as Christ was crucified). The idea is that the Holy Spirit strengthens us so that there can be more of Christ in us, and less of us in us.

2. To enable them to truly understand the capacity of God's love. As Christ dwells in us and we are growing in Him we begin to see that God's love is endless. It surpasses knowledge - we can't know the end of it. If we are growing in this understanding then there is no end to our development either; and consequently we begin to experience the nature of

the eternal life we are called to. In making this prayer, Paul wants them to be filled to the brim with the things of God (love, joy, peace, understanding, etc.).

Doxology

> [20] Now to Him who is able to do far more abundantly beyond all that we ask or think, according to the power that works within us, [21] to Him be the glory in the church and in Christ Jesus to all generations forever and ever. Amen.

A doxology refers to spontaneous praise. Paul is praying for them, explaining what blessings they have and, in the middle of it is so overcome by the grace and wonder of it all - he breaks out in praise. He praises God who, he says: is able to do more than we ask, think or even imagine (salvation through Christ; who could have even imagined such a thing?). God is also able to answer prayer beyond our wildest imaginations using what we already possess. In this passage of spontaneous praise we see that: God is glorified and praised by His church, God is glorified and praised only in connection with Christ, and God is glorified and praised in this way forever.

Summary

We are this church today! He's talking about and to us as well. We are the instrument that delivers the message of salvation in the 21st century. We have the Word and Spirit today. Paul's prayer should be our prayer: more of Christ in us, and that the roots of God's love grow deep within us. Instead of asking for more things, more time, more comfort, we should ask God to expand our capacity to be filled with spiritual blessings. In other words, ask Him to give us a better taste of the world to come, not the world we're in.

7.
UNITY OF THE CHURCH

EPHESIANS 4:1-16

Paul begins by praying that God opens the Ephesian church's eyes so that they will be better able to appreciate the blessings of salvation. He describes the hopeless situation of the Gentiles in the past and the glory that they now have as equal partners with the Jews as brothers in Christ and members of His body, the church. He teaches them that salvation and their inclusion into the kingdom was a plan God kept secret from the beginning (even the angels did not know the full details). He also explains that God now uses the church as the medium for the revelation of this good news to all creation in heaven and on earth. Finally, he prays that God expand their capacity to receive Christ into their hearts so that they will be totally possessed and filled with His love. With this idea we end the second main part of the letter dealing with the universal nature of the church and move into a discussion of the church's obligations.

So far Paul has described in great detail the things that God has done for them through Christ. In the final section the Apostle will review the response that God expects from the church. This includes three obligations that the church has in response to God's wonderful plan of salvation and provision for His people. The first of these is the need to preserve unity, and Paul will use up this entire chapter speaking on this point.

The Call to Unity

> [1] Therefore I, the prisoner of the Lord, implore you to walk in a manner worthy of the calling with which you have been called, [2] with all humility and gentleness, with patience, showing tolerance for one another in love, [3] being diligent to preserve the unity of the Spirit in the bond of peace.

He begins by exhorting them to preserve the unity that already exists, and to which they (the church) were added. The church does not create unity; unity already exists between the Father, Son and the Holy Spirit. When Jesus gave His life to create the church, His word to instruct it, and the Holy Spirit to sustain it, He made the church part of this unified Godhead ("That they may be in us." - John 17:21). Jesus is part of the divine and unified Godhead, and the church through the cross, the word and the Holy Spirit is part of Jesus. Therefore the church is also (through its connection to Jesus) part of the unified Godhead. Every person (Jew or Gentile) who becomes part of the church also becomes part of the unified Godhead.

Jesus, as Paul has explained, has maintained his unity with the Father and Holy Spirit by accomplishing the plan of salvation. Paul explains what the church must do in order to maintain its unity with Christ because disunity in the church equals disunity with Christ and the Godhead; this is why unity is such an important issue. The threat of division among the Ephesians also threatened the loss of unity with Christ. And so, Paul begins this section by encouraging them to preserve unity and he explains how they are to do this.

Preserving the unity in the church requires that we have a certain attitude towards one another, and Paul explains what this attitude should be. It begins with humility, a virtue that is the opposite of pride and vanity. A humble person has an accurate assessment of self. Another similar attitude is that of meekness. One who is meek does not constantly seek his own will, and is not violent. Paul mentions the quality of patience, so necessary to maintain unity and peace in any organization, not only in the church. A patient person is one who is willing to put up with trials, suffering, failure and the offenses of others without losing control or cheerfulness. He finishes this list by mentioning forbearance, which is the ability to not be easily provoked to anger or discouragement by the actions of others.

Paul tells them that in Christ both Jews and Gentiles are equally blessed, saved and precious to God. He tells them that by practicing humility, patience, meekness and forbearance with one another they will be able to preserve the unity into which they entered when Jesus brought them into the church.

The Basis of Unity

> [4] There is one body and one Spirit, just as also you were called in one hope of your calling; [5] one Lord, one faith, one baptism, [6] one God and Father of all who is over all and through all and in all.

Many times we confuse unity with conformity. Conformity is sameness. We become the same as something or someone else (i.e. McDonald's restaurants serve the same tasting foods no matter where you go). Unity, on the other hand, is the experience of sharing. We share a similar hope, leader and ideals. The sharing of these becomes the basis of our unity, not the effort to all be the same. In verses 4-6, Paul will mention seven objectives that the Ephesians share and in so doing brings them into union with one another and God.

1. One body – There is only one group of saved; one church in God's eyes.

2. One Spirit – The Holy Spirit; His work and influence.

3. One hope – Salvation and its effects.

4. One Lord – Jesus (there is no other by which we are saved – Acts 4:12).

5. One faith – The teachings of Jesus and the Apostles.

6. One baptism – There is only one baptism (immersion in water in the name of Jesus – Acts 2:38) that puts us into the one body, gives us one spirit, permits one hope, unites us to one Lord and taught by one faith.

7. One God – Creator of heaven and earth. The God of Abraham, Isaac and Jacob. The One who sent Jesus.

Paul's point is that these things (beliefs, responses on our part) unite us to Christ, to God and to one another. They are at the center and hold us together as one. For example, in the "one" baptism I am united to Christ, and through Him to God and the Holy Spirit, but also to everyone else who has experienced the same baptism. Of course, the opposite is true as well, to be divided from these things is also to be divided from Christ and each other. So, maintaining the unity that exists in the church requires a right type of attitude towards one another and a sharing of the elements of our faith (body, spirit, hope, Lord, faith, baptism, God).

God Helps us Keep Unity

> [7] But to each one of us grace was given according to the measure of Christ's gift. [8] Therefore it says,
>
> "When He ascended on high,
> He led captive a host of captives,
> And He gave gifts to men."

> [9] (Now this expression, "He ascended," what does it mean except that He also had descended into the lower parts of the earth? [10] He who descended is Himself also He who ascended far above all the heavens, so that He might fill all things.) [11] And He gave some as apostles, and some as prophets, and some as evangelists, and some as pastors and teachers, [12] for the equipping of the saints for the work of service, to the building up of the body of Christ; [13] until we all attain to the unity of the faith, and of the knowledge of the Son of God, to a mature man, to the measure of the stature which belongs to the fullness of Christ.

Of course, we are not alone in our effort to maintain unity, God helps us with certain gifts that He provides. At this point Paul describes a set that we rarely perceive as "gifts." In regards to this unity and the maintaining of it, each person has received a gift (grace) in order to contribute to the unity that already exists (verses 7-10). This grace has been given by Christ to each, and given according to His ability (or fullness) to give out these gifts. And just how "able" is Jesus to give gifts? Paul quotes an Old Testament Psalm (Psalms 68:18) that summarizes Christ's achievements on behalf of men: He has died and gone to the underworld, He has resurrected and ascended to the right hand of God. His presence fills both the spiritual and physical realms. The point is that Jesus is supremely able to supply abundantly the "gifts" needed to maintain this unity of the Spirit in the bond of peace.

Paul then explains that the gifts he is talking about here are not different kinds of powers, but in fact are people! And each is a gift in two ways: first there is the enabling and empowering from God to carry out some kind of ministry as one of these servants, and then the blessing one receives as you receive the gift of ministry from these people. Either way, they are the gifts that help the church maintain unity.

The gifts he mentions are:

1. The Apostles – These were messengers chosen by Christ to witness the resurrection, establish the church and record the New Testament so that we can continue teaching the church to know and obey all the commands of Christ today (Matthew 28:18-20).

2. Prophets – There were different types of prophets. Old Testament prophets like Isaiah counseled kings and foretold of future events concerning the nation of Israel and the coming of the Messiah (Isaiah 53:1-12). New Testament prophets also foretold the future (i.e. Agabus, Acts 21:10-11) but in addition to this they served the church by teaching God's word before the New Testament record was compiled and organized. Today we have the complete revelation of God's word in the Bible and no longer have need for inspired prophets. This ministry is now carried out by preachers and teachers who use the inspired word of God to preach the gospel, warn of the judgment to come and teach the church the will and purpose of God.

3. Evangelists – These men proclaimed the gospel (i.e. Phillip, Acts 8). They also established and organized congregations as well as promoted unity (i.e. epistles to Timothy and Titus).

4. Pastors and teachers – Elders who shepherd by teaching (Acts 20). Those who teach the word but don't shepherd (Acts 13).

These servants of the church are gifts (even today) because their role and abilities come from God. Their work consists of building up the church and maintaining that unity that Paul speaks of at the beginning of the chapter. They do this by supplying each saint what he or she needs to serve others in the body. Their goal is to achieve perfect unity in Christ by cultivating the following: unity of faith by helping others grow in their knowledge of and trust in Christ; unity of relationships by establishing correct priorities (i.e. Christ first, others, then self); unity of service by growing in the ability to share the gospel and express love to God and others. Christ gives these people to the church so they will serve the church in helping it mature in every phase of unity.

Results of Unity

> ^{14} As a result, we are no longer to be children, tossed here and there by waves and carried about by every wind of doctrine, by the trickery of men, by craftiness in deceitful scheming; ^{15} but speaking the truth in love, we are to grow up in all aspects into Him who is the head, even Christ, ^{16} from whom the whole body, being fitted and held together by what every joint supplies, according to the proper working of each individual part, causes the growth of the body for the building up of itself in love.

One result of unity is being firmly planted in the word and not being easily seduced by lies, tricks, and the plans of evil men and Satan. Another is speaking the truth in love. This type of speech has no patience with gossip, divisiveness or hypocrisy, but excels in the ability to speak the word to the lost and those who are struggling. Another product of unity is maturity in Christ. We become like Jesus in our attitude and character, and this strengthens our unity with God and each other. Finally, unity promotes cooperation in mutual service. The body functions in the way the head directs for the strengthening of every member. The idea is that the body is to grow to the point of maturity that the head has already accomplished (we become like Jesus, perfectly united to God and each other). God provides key agents (gifts) in the body to help every part grow towards this ideal.

Summary

Of course, like conformity, there is also a downside to the pursuit of unity. The cost of unity is discomfort! It is not easy maintaining love, patience, gentleness and forbearance with someone you disagree with about the one Lord, faith, baptism, etc. That is why conformity is so appealing (everybody agrees or they are out, and it's easy to get along with people who agree with you). But God says that we need to make an effort to maintain unity through peace since He knew it would not be easy because we are not all at the same maturity level, we have been taught different things, we are sinful and our sins limit our understanding. In many instances we have misunderstood what we have been taught, and we have prejudices as well. Because of these things we find it difficult to get along, to be patient and loving towards those who don't agree with us. But making the effort to maintain unity despite these obstacles is the true test of our discipleship because Jesus said, "Your love for one another will prove to the world that you are my disciples" (John 13:35).

Notice that He didn't say:

- How big a group you are will prove...
- That you are all the same will prove...
- That you know all the doctrines will prove...
- That you think you're right will prove...
- That you're very motivated will prove...

All those who have confessed Christ and have been buried in baptism have been added to a divinely united circle that includes the Father, Son, Holy Spirit and the church. The greatest task we have as Christians is to maintain that unity and that oneness by loving one another despite our differences.

8.
THE RESPONSE OF RIGHTEOUSNESS

EPHESIANS 4:17-5:14

Chapter 4:1 summarizes the first three chapters of the letter and serves as a turning point to establish the context of the balance of Paul's message. In this verse he reaches back to summarize everything he has already said: he's prayed that God enables them to experience and grow in appreciation of the blessings they have in Christ, he reminds them of God's great love in saving them (the Gentiles) when they were completely separated from God, and God Himself called them and now uses them to reveal His plan to angels and men. Paul continues the chapter by saying that since these things are true and have been done on their behalf, they should live in such a way that these truths are evident to others. The obligations of this new life, this life as the church of Christ, are then explained in the balance of the letter.

In the previous chapter we looked at the first of these obligations that was to maintain the unity that Christ had established. Christ established this unity by creating and drawing to Himself the church that would become united to God through Him. Christ enabled the church to maintain this unity by providing apostles, prophets, evangelists, pastors and teachers to help the church mature in the knowledge of and service to Christ and one another. The basis of this unity was expressed in the seven elements that every individual member of the church shared with every other member regardless of culture or time. Each member equally shared the same: body (they were part of one church), Spirit (they received the same Holy Spirit), hope (they looked forward to heaven), Lord (they all submitted to Jesus only), faith (they taught the same doctrine), baptism (they each experienced the same immersion in water for the same reasons), Father (all called on the God of creation, the God of Abraham, Isaac, and Jacob; the One who sent Jesus). The pursuit of these elements of unity was the first obligation of the church because this is what kept it part of Christ.

Righteousness

> [17] So this I say, and affirm together with the Lord, that you walk no longer just as the Gentiles also walk, in the futility of their mind, [18] being darkened in their understanding, excluded from the life of God because of the ignorance that is in them, because of the hardness of their heart; [19] and they, having become callous, have given themselves over to sensuality for the practice of every kind of impurity with greediness. [20] But you did not learn Christ in this way, [21] if indeed you have heard Him and have been taught in Him, just as truth is in Jesus, [22] that, in reference to your former manner of life, you lay aside the old self, which is being corrupted in accordance with the lusts of deceit, [23] and that you be renewed in the spirit of your mind, [24] and put on the new self, which in the likeness of God has been created in righteousness and holiness of the truth.

The second obligation Paul speaks of is the need to be righteous or holy. The church is holy because God is holy; the church is righteous because God is righteous. To be righteous/holy means that you conduct yourself in a particular way, you react to things in a special way.

Paul begins explaining this idea with a comparison. He says that the Christian does not act like the non-Christian. Non-Christians (pagans) walk according to what is in their minds or what they have learned. The problem is that what is in their minds is false and will not lead them to salvation - no matter how long they live. Because they lack the knowledge of the truth, their walk is characterized by several things: misunderstanding, godlessness, ignorance, hard hearts (they don't care about what is good), sensuality, impurity, and the never-ending appetite for more (greed), more evil, more things. Paul explains that these things are prevalent in their lives.

The comparison he makes is to the mind of the Christian. The one who is a member of Christ's church has his mind full of the word of God. Because he thinks this way (having been taught by the one faith) he has escaped the consequences facing the Gentile, which is corruption (death). A believer's walk, because of this knowledge, is holy, just and true. Because he has been transformed (by the one Lord, one Spirit, the one hope, etc.) his manner of walking has also been transformed. The image is one of removing an old beggar's coat that identifies you as such and putting on a prince's cloak that completely transforms how you feel about yourself and how others see and feel about you. That new covering is Christ, and what others see is not the human form of Jesus but His righteousness in the way you think, speak and act. So Paul says that the church is obliged not to live as the pagans live, but rather live like Christ would live. This new "righteous or holy" lifestyle has several recognizable features.

The Features of a Righteous Life

A proper attitude toward others

> [25] Therefore, laying aside falsehood, speak truth each one of you with his neighbor, for we are members of one another. [26] Be angry, and yet do

> not sin; do not let the sun go down on your anger, ²⁷ and do not give the devil an opportunity. ²⁸ He who steals must steal no longer; but rather he must labor, performing with his own hands what is good, so that he will have something to share with one who has need. ²⁹ Let no unwholesome word proceed from your mouth, but only such a word as is good for edification according to the need of the moment, so that it will give grace to those who hear. ³⁰ Do not grieve the Holy Spirit of God, by whom you were sealed for the day of redemption. ³¹ Let all bitterness and wrath and anger and clamor and slander be put away from you, along with all malice. ³² Be kind to one another, tender-hearted, forgiving each other, just as God in Christ also has forgiven you.

In this section Paul gives a list (not a complete one) of attitudes that immediately identify one who is of the household of faith. This person lives righteously; this type of life is full of sincerity (being honest with everyone about everything, because dishonesty breaks ties, destroys unity in a marriage, in a friendship and especially in the church). Paul continues his list by mentioning peacefulness; it is impossible to avoid anger, but a child of God always works towards peace as a first priority. Not letting the sun go down on your anger doesn't mean you have to get "closure" before the end of the day; this is an expression that means to not let anger go on beyond its "time." Another feature of the righteous life is a sense of responsibility; in other words, a faithful Christian is known for being a giver not a taker. Saints work to give and share with others, not simply to hoard what they have been given by God.

Finally, Paul mentions gracious speech and mercy as two other hallmarks of a righteous life. The Holy Spirit is given to us to help us grow and serve others in their efforts to grow in unity and love. When the church is involved in bitterness, anger, exasperation, strife and harsh speech against others, it frustrates the work of the Spirit (grieves). Disappointments and offenses are bound to rise up but the proper response for the church is mercy, forgiveness, kindness, always remembering that this is the way God treated the church. And so, the first recognizable feature of righteousness is the way the members treat each other in the church. Jesus said, "This is how all men will know you are my disciples, in the way you love one another." John 13:35

A higher quality of life - 5:1-14

In the previous paragraph Paul focused on relationships and how righteous people were to treat each other. In chapter five he will target the Christian's personal conduct and how this conduct must rise above an unbeliever's conduct if it is to be seen as righteous.

Paul summarizes the previous section by compressing everything down to one word: love. He says that if you love (by treating others with mercy, gracious speech, etc.) then you are walking like Christ. And if Christ's life was like a pleasing sacrifice to God, then your imitation of Him in your own life will also be a similar sweet offering to God. In the following verses he will show how very different a Christian's conduct is from unbelievers. Paul likens the difference between the two as the difference between light and dark.

There should not even be a suggestion that improper things are happening among you (i.e. fornication, impurity and greed). Avoid things that appear or may be interpreted as being unworthy of someone who is a saint. When saints are together they must not act like the Gentiles but rather act like saints; this is not hypocrisy. We are hypocrites if we act like the world when in reality we are saints.

He talks about three things: filthiness (indecency), silly talk (empty talk, devoid of the truth/superstition), and coarse jesting (dirty or nasty talk). Paul says that these things have no place among those who call themselves holy. These things are not of saints but of Gentiles, and you know that the Gentiles are damned. Paul warns them not to be talked into participation because it is for these very kinds of sins that God will punish the Gentiles. His point is that if they participate with them, they will also participate with them in the punishment. The Apostle calls on them to remember who they were (when pressured to participate in deeds of the flesh). They were children of God, not meant to produce darkness but light (righteousness, goodness, truth). On the contrary, he tells them to find ways to please the Lord, not how to grieve the Spirit. He encourages them to be aggressive and expose their evil and rebuke their sins that are too shameful to mention. If they are the light then they must not hide the light of truth, but rather use it to bring everything into the light! There are many different ideas here but one idea is that when you bring the deeds of darkness into the light, it is the motivation for sinners to become children of light themselves.

Verse 14 explores an early Christian poem or song expressing the power of the light of Christ on the sinner and will summarize what Paul has said in this section. He explains that righteousness is also evident from personal conduct that is in direct contrast to the world and, thus, serves as a witness to its sinfulness. The saved are special and walk differently. They walk in unity. They walk in holiness and righteousness. That righteousness is noticeable in that it is a complete transformation from the old way of life. It has certain features: it is filled with kindness, compassion, forgiveness and love towards others. It is a life lived in the light of Christ without even a suggestion of impurity in words or actions. This type of living inevitably lights up all the darkness around it thereby creating light where there was darkness. In the next chapter we will examine more features of this righteousness.

9.
TRUE PIETY

EPHESIANS 5:15-21

Paul explains that the church has, as a response to God's gracious offer of blessings, certain responsibilities and obligations. God invites all mankind (no distinctions) to receive precious spiritual blessings that He has reserved in heaven. In response to this, those who receive these blessings are obliged to live a certain way. So far, we've seen that one of these obligations is that the church preserve the unity that God has established by making the church part of the Godhead through Christ. Another obligation is to live righteously, and Paul explains that two features of this righteous lifestyle include a loving attitude toward others and a life that is holy and beyond reproach by the world. We will now examine other elements of this righteous lifestyle that Paul began describing in chapter 4:17 and will continue doing so until chapter 6:9 of his letter to the Ephesian church.

Features of a Righteous Lifestyle

Piety

The dictionary defines piety as "actions that show devotion or reverence for God." A pious person is a person for whom the things of God, or the activities connected with God, are very important. Of course there is great danger in this area because some use false piety as a cover for sin (i.e. television evangelists who pray, sweat and cry but are only interested in fleecing their followers of their money), or people who fight over every little tradition defending piety when what they really want is to get their own way. In the Bible, the Pharisees were the worst offenders in this area. Their many rules and traditions created the image of piety when in reality their hearts were not truly turned towards God.

It is easy to look pious but not so easy to be truly pious. Paul encourages the Ephesians towards true piety in bringing together the features of Christian piety. In other words, he coaches them on how to sincerely express their devotion to God and His affairs. The way to true Christian piety lay in the following:

Be prudent

> [15] Therefore be careful how you walk, not as unwise men but as wise, [16] making the most of your time, because the days are evil. [17] So then do not be foolish, but understand what the will of the Lord is.

Be careful how you live your life; don't take chances with your soul and the precious blessings that have been freely given to you in Christ. He doesn't mention anything specific that they must do. Prudence is an attitude that weighs the various options in life and their effect upon the blessings that they possess in Christ. Christians know the truth about life and death and the hereafter so their lives are lived in this context. Unlike foolish men who are not aware of this and have nothing to guard except the few material possessions they may have accumulated here on earth. The prudent person, who knows the truth, seeks the will of the Lord for his life, and makes the most of his short time here on earth because he knows the judgment is coming, and this world is evil; so he's careful and prudent. If piety is a concern for Godly things, then the pious person is first and foremost prudent about how he lives making sure that his life is in accord with God's will. This is not religious hypocrisy or a holier than thou attitude, this is a sober realization that God exercises both His mercy and His judgment, and one must live in accordance with this reality.

Be spirit filled

> [18] And do not get drunk with wine, for that is dissipation, but be filled with the Spirit, [19] speaking to one another in psalms and hymns and spiritual songs, singing and making melody with your heart to the Lord; [20] always giving thanks for all things in the name of our Lord Jesus Christ to God, even the Father;

False piety is usually full of religious looking activities that look very spiritual, but as Paul says in Colossians 2:23, "…have no value against fleshly indulgence." In other words, superficial religion has no effect on changing or renewing a person's spirit. True piety, true devotion to the things of God, is seen when one's true devotion is to Christ and the things that Christ has given. The pagans and religious phonies stir up their spirits with alcohol; this is not true spirituality, this does not build up the individual or the body. Actually, this destroys both. Instead of being filled with the stupefying spirit of alcohol and such things, be filled with the regenerating power of the Holy Spirit. This is what the will of the Lord is, that those concerned with the things of God be filled with the Holy Spirit and witness that they are.

You can make an even more general application of this idea. You can be filled with (addicted to) a lot of things in life: leisure, money, career, pleasure, power, comfort, drugs, etc. What you are filled with will be evident because that is what you will talk about, worry about and be involved in the most. But if you are prudent, in the short time you have here, you will be filled with the spirit, and that fullness of spirit will be evident because much of your time and effort aside from earning a living and family life will be invested in Bible study. How else can we know the will of the Lord? Those who attend as many studies as they can are not only zealous, they are prudent and wise and know how to invest in the treasures that last forever. The life filled with the spirit will overflow in joyful praise expressed in songs, hymns and psalms. Singing isn't a duty, it is an expression and an overflow of what's inside!

Giving thanks for all things is also evidence, "it was because of lack of thanksgiving that the wise became fools and fell into darkness." Romans 1:21

Many times we are conned into confusing emotionalism or modernism with spirituality. If we feel excited or entertained, if we're impressed with size or lights and performance, we're led to believe that this experience is spiritual. But Paul explains that true spirituality in someone's life will be seen in knowledge and obedience of God's word; joyful praise and sincere gratitude for His kindness. With this criteria every Christian and every congregation can be filled with the Spirit, regardless of size or resources.

Be subject to one another

> [21] and be subject to one another in the fear of Christ.

True piety involves a particular attitude towards other people, and Paul describes the pious person as one who is able to subject himself to others. This word (subject) comes from the same root word used later on in Ephesians 5:22 (wives be subject/submit to your husbands). To be "subject" was a military term which meant to "place oneself under." It literally meant that a soldier would recognize another soldier of a higher rank and accept that person's superior rank and put themselves under that person's command. Paul says this should be everyone's attitude in the church. The question arises, "Well, how does the church function with this attitude since there are clearly roles of higher and lower responsibility and authority (i.e. elders, Hebrews 13:17 "...obey your leaders, submit to them...").

A person can still function in a leadership role and have a submissive attitude. Jesus was Lord of all, and yet He submitted to the Father's will, submitted to the weakness and needs of those He served and submitted to the limitations placed upon Him by His human nature. A mutually submissive attitude for everyone in the church does not eliminate leadership responsibilities or lines of authority, however, this kind of attitude does eliminate pride, rivalry and the desire of the approval of men, all of which are causes of dissention and disputes in the church.

A pious elder will see himself as a shepherd and a protector of the church, not its lord and master. A pious deacon will bear patiently with the weaknesses of his brothers and sisters instead of complaining about their deficiencies. And all will support the leadership of those appointed to that task without grumbling or jealousy knowing that their task is difficult and they need help, not criticism. A truly pious person is one who emulates the character of Jesus and His approach to dealing with people and problems. This approach begins with the willingness to submit to others' needs, weaknesses and positions for the glory of the church. This was the way the church began, Jesus subjecting Himself to a death on the cross. This is how the church continues, each member dies to self and lives for Christ.

Summary

We are reviewing the various features of a righteous lifestyle, which is one of the obligations of the church in response to the blessings God has given it. We've looked at three features of that righteous lifestyle that Paul describes: a loving attitude, a lifestyle that is beyond reproach and piety of character (prudence, Spirit filled and submissive). Note that in our day and age, to be tender-hearted and loving; to be beyond reproach in our lifestyle; to be careful, spiritually minded and submissive, this is not exactly the ideal man/woman for the 21st century. Christians have always gone against the grain and it is no different today in our generation.

10.
AN ORDERED LIFE

EPHESIANS 5:22-6:9

We're looking at the obligations of the church in response to God's offer of spiritual blessings to all who come to Jesus. These included the pursuit of unity and personal righteousness. We are in the process of studying the various features of the righteous lifestyle described in chapters 4:17-6:19. So far, Paul has described three of these: a loving attitude, a life beyond reproach and piety which is best seen in the virtue of prudence, and the practice of spirit filled living and submissiveness among the brothers and sisters in the church. At this point let us look at the fourth element of righteousness described by Paul, an ordered life.

The three previous features had to do with a person's individual character and attitude. This last feature describes the Christian's relationship with family and society. When it comes to these, God has established a desired order according to His will.

Orderly Family

> [22] Wives, be subject to your own husbands, as to the Lord. [23] For the husband is the head of the wife, as Christ also is the head of the church, He Himself being the Savior of the body.

Paul begins with the description of the orderly family because it is the basic unit in society. If there is disorder here, there is disorder in society. Paul does not cover every detail of a woman's role in marriage; instead he establishes the one attitude that will guide all others. Wives should submit to their husbands (military term meaning to rank under, to yield). Wives are to do this voluntarily because it is not a question of superiority, it is a question of faith (obeying God).

Paul says that in the same way you submit to Christ, submit also to your husband. One can't be done without the other. Paul also answers the question, "why is this necessary?" The answer is that God has given the leadership role in the family to the husband, just as He has made Christ the head of the church. There can only be one head, just as there can be one body. God has created marriage in such a way that it is an instructional copy of the relationship between Christ and the church.

That a wife willingly submits to her husband is a spiritual idea not grasped by the carnal mind, nor the world in general. The point Paul makes is that when this takes place, it creates harmony between what is seen and what is not seen in the spiritual world.

Of course, this is not always possible where the husband is dead, the husband is an unbeliever, and/or abusive, the husband refuses leadership, or the wife is evil/refuses role/etc. Just as other things mentioned (loving attitude, piety, etc.), submissiveness is a goal one strives for through practice and prayer, but it should be a goal for all Christian wives.

Some say that this was a social thing in the first century, not valid for today, but Paul confirms: the church has this relationship with Christ forever. In the same way, so long as there is the marriage relationship (until we are in heaven) this is the way God intends for it to remain. Marriage will always reflect the church. There is no confusion, the wife should be prepared to yield completely to her husband.

This is what young women should consider before marrying, "is this the kind of man I would be willing to submit to? (Not just where we would live, work, wedding dress, etc.) Am I willing to put my life into his hands?" If you are not willing to do this then don't marry this person!

This is a major cause of marital conflict and divorce: the confusion of the roles within the marriage. Some have the attitude that says, "I will submit only when and where I feel like it. I want my independence." The mistake in thinking like this is the fact that there is NO independence in marriage! Marriage is the opposite of independence; it is a mutually dependent state where each partner strives to serve the other in love. Of course, some reject this notion of submissiveness because they are afraid of abuse and with good cause. Abuse comes from sinful men who do not understand their role in Christian marriage. This is why you should only consider marrying a faithful Christian.

This brings us to husbands. Again, Paul mentions only one thing about them but it describes the attitude towards their wives that will set the "tone" for the entire relationship. Love your wives!

Love has many expressions and words that describe it. In the Greek language, which is the original language of the New Testament, there are various Greek words that are translated into the English word "love." For example, the Greek word "eros" refers to love in a sensual way; sexual love, the love of art and music are described by this word. The Greek word "phileos," on the other hand, describes the non-sexual love that two friends might share, or the emotion that drives philanthropic giving. Another Greek word, "storgos" describes the love that exists between family members. Now these three types of love exist in most marriages and describe how relationships evolve.

However, the word that Paul uses to describe the love that a man must have for his wife is the Greek word "agapao," a word that describes the type of love that is sacrificial in nature, and in the next verses he gives Jesus as the example of this kind of sacrificial love. Jesus' love for his bride, the church, included: His death to save her, His teachings to guarantee her life, and His care to completely purify her and give her an irrevocable position next to Him in heaven.

Every husband has a degree of sensuality, friendliness and sense of belonging in a family, but for his attitude to be raised to a spiritual level, there needs to exist a readiness to love his wife in a sacrificial way. This is what Christ demands of husbands in a marriage. Why? Because in the marriage the two become one, and when a man loves his wife he is loving himself.

Again, Christ is the example. As the head of the church, He loves and cares for the body in all patience, tenderness and necessary sacrifice. That is why the church happily submits to Jesus. This is what young men should look for and consider before they marry: is the girl ready to submit to him in marriage? Is he prepared to provide leadership? Is he able to sacrifice himself for her? Provide for her and family, place her needs before his own, and able to treat her as a special gift from God, give her honor and respect? Or, does he only want her because she will satisfy his needs (especially sexually), take care of his home (spoil him), and replace his mother? If men knew how to be the head of their wives as Christ is head of the church, women would happily submit themselves to their leadership.

Paul summarizes God's plan for orderliness in marriage. The original plan requires that the couple stop relying on their parents and begin relying on each other. It also demands that the marriage be contracted as one man and one woman faithfully married to one another for life. This model for marriage is heavenly in nature because it reflects the union that Christ has with His church. Within that relationship the basic attitudes are: the wife submits to her husband in all things, and the husband loves his wife with a sacrificial love as he loves himself.

Paul has spoken to wives and husbands, and now addresses the third part in the family unit: the children. Order in a family requires that the mothers and fathers maintain certain attitudes and rules, and that children obey these rules. Again, Paul doesn't give all the details about the children's role and obligations, just the basic one found in the Old Testament. This is a variation of the commandment in Exodus 20:12. Children are to obey their parents (because of the Lord and according to the Lord). The obedience to parents is limited to those things that the Lord would require. In Exodus the promise is that those who do obey would have a long life in the Promised Land. Paul revises this promise so that it will include Gentiles.

Paul then adds an exhortation to fathers in the way they bring up their children. The command for children to obey is tempered with an appeal to fathers not to use their authority in such a way as to provoke their children to become angry or discouraged. Children have feelings and to provoke them to helpless anger is wrong. Instead, Paul says that fathers should raise their children according to the discipline and teachings of Christ.

In those days the father had the power of life and death over their young ones, and the children had no rights. Paul urges fathers to actually direct the upbringing of their children according to the practice and teaching of Jesus, and not according to the social customs of the time or their personal whims. The same holds true for today where the cardinal sin of fathers is not harshness or cruelty, but neglect and a poor example. So Paul concludes his instructions for an orderly family by stating that the duty of children is to obey parents, and that of fathers is to lead in the raising of children.

This is contrary to the pattern we too often see in today's society where the wife and mother becomes a type of matriarch, and dominates both her husband and children contrary to God's will.

Orderly Society - Ephesians 6

As I mentioned before, the fourth requirement of righteousness is ordered living and Paul breaks this into two main components: ordered families and ordered society. A righteous man or woman will strive to pattern his/her family according to the order that Christ provides in His word. That same person will also strive to pattern his position in society according to the will of Christ as well. In these few verses, Paul will explain the responsibility of the two main positions within the society of that era: masters and slaves. He will show that regardless of one's position in society (master/slave), a righteous person conducts himself in the order that Christ has given.

Slaves

> [5] Slaves, be obedient to those who are your masters according to the flesh, with fear and trembling, in the sincerity of your heart, as to Christ; [6] not by way of eyeservice, as men-pleasers, but as slaves of Christ, doing the will of God from the heart. [7] With good will render service, as to the Lord, and not to men, [8] knowing that whatever good thing each one does, this he will receive back from the Lord, whether slave or free.

Again, Paul does not give all the details concerning the life and work of a slave. There were various classes of slaves in that society, and each had their own degree of responsibility. The key ingredient Paul urged them to cultivate was "sincere obedience." This required them to obey with the knowledge that their masters were masters of only their bodies, not their souls.

He instructs them to obey with respect and with the same enthusiasm that they would obey Christ. They were not to act as hypocrites towards their masters by feigning outward submissiveness while despising them in their hearts. Paul says that they should obey with sincere good will knowing that serving in this way fulfills the will of God in this matter, and that God will reward both slave and master in the end.

Paul doesn't promote or defend slavery (I Corinthians 7:21), he simply gives those in that position the way to live so as to please the Lord, and in doing so demonstrate their righteousness, even as slaves. In the end, history demonstrates that the rise and practice of Christianity, and not open rebellion, did away with slavery in most countries.

Masters

> ^{9} And masters, do the same things to them, and give up threatening, knowing that both their Master and yours is in heaven, and there is no partiality with Him.

Paul finishes with a word to masters. There were Christians who owned slaves in those days (i.e. Philemon). This was the structure of that society. A "household" included family and slaves as part of one unit. To the masters Paul gives one reminder and that is that everyone (slave or master) has the same "Master" in heaven who will judge all. A judge who will not be favorable to one or the other. All will be judged according to the same standard and righteousness according to God's word. If this is so, then they should stop using coercion and violence to motivate their slaves. Again, an attitude of fairness and respect carried over to today's employees. The unsaid idea is that they should use what the Master uses to motivate us: kindness, teaching, encouragement, generosity and not just authority.

Summary

With this, Paul completes the information concerning the final elements required in order to live a righteous life before God, an ordered life in one's family and society. He will complete this section by explaining one more obligation that the church has in response to God's blessings: faithfulness.

11. FAITHFULNESS

EPHESIANS 6:10-24

Paul describes the blessings God has prepared for the church and offers thanks to God for these. He goes on to explain that these are available for both Jews and Gentiles who come to Christ. He finishes his letter by outlining the response or obligations God seeks from the church because of these blessings. These obligations require the church to live righteously and this is seen in a loving attitude, a holy and pious lifestyle, and last of all: faithfulness, which is the subject of this concluding chapter.

The Enemy and the Battle Plan

> [10] Finally, be strong in the Lord and in the strength of His might. [11] Put on the full armor of God, so that you will be able to stand firm against the schemes of the devil. [12] For our struggle is not against flesh and blood, but against the rulers, against the powers, against the world forces of this darkness, against the spiritual forces of wickedness in the heavenly places. [13] Therefore, take up the full armor of God, so that you will be able to resist in the evil day, and having done everything, to stand firm.

In the final section of this letter, Paul will use the image of a Roman soldier to explain how Christians are to remain faithful. This is a departure from his style in the rest of the letter, which explains in theological and practical terms the life and responsibility of Christians. Paul finishes his letter, however, with high imagery and an enthusiastic call to arms in rallying the church to remain faithful.

His call is to "be strong" with the strength of God, not the strength of man. He repeats the same idea twice for emphasis. The strength or power is not about bulging muscles or human fighting skills; it is about using the strength of God for the battle. In these verses, Paul explains that it is the strength of God that is necessary since the enemy is not human but spiritual in nature (6:11-13).

The readers would have understood the imagery of "full armor" to refer to the Roman line soldier, the fully armored legionnaire with whom Rome conquered other nations. In the same way that these soldiers were fully covered, Paul says that Christians should be fully covered with God's armor. This is the strength that God provides for us. Paul also says that once covered, the Christian needs to stand firm (immovable, invincible) against the expert attack of the enemy because he is not a mere man, he is the devil himself.

Paul describes the battle as a struggle that suggests hand-to-hand combat. No long-range artillery here, everyone is on the line face to face with the enemy. No ordinary wrestling match where you lose points, but a hand to hand struggle for life and death. He goes on to give two views of the opposing spiritual army. One is of the evil rulers/powers/forces led by Satan, and the other is of a great number of wicked spirits.

The exhortation is to put on all of God's armor because human strength cannot prevail against such an enemy. In the end, the last one standing will be the victor. There will be a battle, it will be a battle to the death, you will be in that battle, and if you remain standing (faithful), you will have the victory.

The Spiritual Armor

He goes on to describe the seven-piece armor of the Christian warrior using the imagery of the Roman soldier getting dressed for battle. Movies have used this "preparation for battle" scene many times to show how the hero readies for the climactic final showdown with the enemy.

Truth

> ¹⁴ᵃ Stand firm therefore, having girded your loins with truth,

The basic tunic was worn by soldiers as a basic garment or covering. To cover oneself with the truth of God is basic because Satan's main weapon is the lie. Truth is the basis for courage, boldness and freedom. The enemy is rendered powerless against the truth (favorite lies: there is no God, you're not good enough).

Righteousness

> ¹⁴ᵇ and having put on the breastplate of righteousness,

This is the metal breastplate worn and strapped over the tunic. The righteousness referred to is that which God gives us because of our faith in Christ. We are acceptable to God because of our faith in Jesus. God's righteousness cannot be pierced, however one of Satan's lethal arrows could easily pierce the thin shield of self-righteousness.

The Gospel

> ¹⁵ and having shod your feet with the preparation of the gospel of peace;

Soldiers wore foot coverings over their sandals that went up their shins. The key word here is "preparation." The thought is that the Christian soldier is prepared to walk into battle on account of the gospel. The gospel is the "power" of God (Romans 1:16) and it is the power that enables the Christian to do battle, to stand firm. The gospel assures the Christian of his salvation and gives him strength to face the enemy who wants to take that away.

The Faith

> [16] in addition to all, taking up the shield of faith with which you will be able to extinguish all the flaming arrows of the evil one.

The Roman soldier had a scutum that was a 4-foot high shield that covered him from his knees to his eyes and provided protection from arrows and other enemy projectiles. The shield of the Christian is not simply the subjective faith that says "I believe as true what the Bible says." The shield is the actual doctrine itself, the actual Word of God that responds to Satan's fiery attacks with "It is written…" This is the shield that Jesus used to defend Himself against Satan's attacks in the desert.

Salvation

> [17a] And take the helmet of salvation,

The soldier wore a helmet as lethal blow protection. He could survive a wound to the leg or arm but a blow to the head was rarely survivable, and so he wore protective head covering. Paul has explained from the start that God has blessed them with all the spiritual blessings that include: forgiveness for all sins, resurrection, glorification and exaltation. In this passage he compresses all of their blessings into one word: salvation. He tells them that the battle will sometimes be fierce and there may be injuries, but so long as they keep the helmet on (confidence that they possess salvation), no mortal blows will be struck.

The Word

> ¹⁷ᵇ and the sword of the Spirit, which is the word of God.

He has described defensive equipment that the soldier must possess, now he goes on to describe two offensive weapons. The Roman soldier usually carried an assortment of weapons. His most basic was the 3-foot sword (gladius) strapped to his side. Paul described the Word of God (the faith) as a defensive weapon in a previous verse referring to it as a shield. Now he changes the imagery to describe God's Word as "the sword of the Spirit" because the Holy Spirit gives us the Word (II Peter 1:21). Man's word, intelligence, will and wisdom will not do in this fight, only God's Word will do. They say you have to fight fire with fire. The same is true here. One has to fight spirit with Spirit: the evil spirits with the Spirit of God.

Prayer

> ¹⁸ With all prayer and petition pray at all times in the Spirit, and with this in view, be on the alert with all perseverance and petition for all the saints, ¹⁹ and pray on my behalf, that utterance may be given to me in the opening of my mouth, to make known with boldness the mystery of the gospel, ²⁰ for which I am an ambassador in chains; that in proclaiming it I may speak boldly, as I ought to speak.

For the soldier, the final preparation for war is mental preparation. A soldier spends many hours in briefings before going on to war games or simulated attacks. The commanders want a soldier to be mentally alert, focused, tough and motivated. If a soldier becomes careless and mentally lazy, he could be easily hurt or killed, even in war games and trial runs.

Paul exhorts the Christians at Ephesus to remain alert by keeping their minds keyed in through prayer: praying consistently, praying in the Spirit, praying for each other and praying for him (that he will also stay in the battle and do his job). The Christian stays focused and in communication with his commander through prayer.

And so, Paul encourages Christians to see themselves in a battle against spiritual forces and tells them to put on all the spiritual armor God provides. A Christian in battle does not try to engage the enemy on his own. He must use the offensive weapons of the Word and prayer to defend against the enemy, and stand firm until the enemy is defeated.

The Training Methods

> [21] But that you also may know about my circumstances, how I am doing, Tychicus, the beloved brother and faithful minister in the Lord, will make everything known to you. [22] I have sent him to you for this very purpose, so that you may know about us, and that he may comfort your hearts.

People learn best when taught by example and so in verses 21-22 Paul provides an example of a soldier in action. The Apostle sends Tychicus to give them a "picture" of Paul's own battle. With his description of Paul's status, Tychicus will give the brethren a vision of Paul, the great spiritual warrior, wearing the armor, using the sword and prayer while engaged at the worst front of battle, a Roman prison. In seeing that the armor works and that he is still standing firm, the Ephesians will be encouraged and comforted in their own struggle.

Salvation

> [23] Peace be to the brethren, and love with faith, from God the Father and the Lord Jesus Christ. [24] Grace be with all those who love our Lord Jesus Christ with incorruptible love.

Paul ends with a blessing. In the beginning, he offered God a prayer of thanks and praise on behalf of the brethren. In the end, the faith, peace and love come from the Father to the brethren thus completing the connection between God and His children. As Paul concludes, his prayer is that this relationship, planned before time began, will now continue after time has come to an end now that the receivers of the blessings (the church) are eternal beings like the giver of blessings, almighty God. To God be the glory in Christ through the Holy Spirit forever, Amen.

Lessons

Here are some final thoughts for our application.

These are our blessings. Everything Paul talked about at the beginning is for us. We have all the blessings of heaven secured for us by God. And these are our responsibilities/obligations. The Holy Spirit, through Paul, speaks to us today about unity, righteousness and faithfulness. These things God continues to expect from us today. This is our battle. We have to be strong, remain standing and put on our armor if we are to stand firm until the end. Each one of us is on the battle line each day in the war against the evil in high places.

APPENDIX A
REVIEW OF RE-BAPTISM

When reviewing the establishment of the church at Ephesus we encounter the often confusing issue of re-baptism as seen in Paul's baptizing the twelve believers who had previously been baptized into John the Baptist's baptism before being taught by Paul. In this chapter I would like to clarify and expand on this topic since there are usually many questions that arise when discussing the issue of re-baptizing a previously baptized believer. In order to anticipate as many questions as I can, I will explain what I believe the Bible teaches concerning John's baptism, Jesus' baptism, and how these affected those individual believers who lived through the period of time when both of these were in effect.

1. John's baptism – Matthew 3:1-6

John preached that the Messiah and His kingdom were coming, and in order to prepare for it, a person was to repent and be immersed (baptized).

2. Jesus received this baptism – Matthew 3:13-15

Jesus had no sins to repent of but as a human being and a Jew He obeyed all things commanded by God, and John's baptism was one of those things.

3. John's disciples became Jesus' disciples – John 1:35-37

As Jesus' public ministry increased John's decreased, and his disciples began to follow Jesus. This was as it should have been; John was there to prepare the way for Christ.

4. Jesus preached John's message – Matthew 4:17

Jesus continued to preach the message of John, and baptize those who responded to this message (John 4:1-2).

5. After the resurrection and ascension the Apostles were to preach the baptism of Jesus – Matthew 28:18-20

The mode of baptism would be the same (immersion) but the reason and results would be different (Acts 2:38). For example:

- John's baptism – prepare for the kingdom.
- Jesus' baptism – actual forgiveness of sins, indwelling of the Holy Spirit.

John's message and baptism prepared people for the forgiveness and indwelling of the Holy Spirit to come (Matthew 3:11).

The Apostles' message and baptism told people that the promise of the kingdom (forgiveness and Holy Spirit) were now available.

6. Some people lived through John, Jesus, Apostles' ministry – Acts 12:12

Some commonly asked questions about the people who lived through John, Jesus and the Apostles' ministry time:

- When were the Apostles baptized? Since most were disciples of John or became disciples of Jesus during John and Jesus' ministries, they received John's baptism (John 1:35-37).

- Were the Apostles re-baptized after Pentecost when Jesus' baptism was preached at Pentecost? Why?

    o No. Because, like Jesus, they had also fulfilled all righteousness (done all that God had commanded concerning this matter) by receiving John's baptism.

    o In other words, if you had been baptized during John's ministry or Jesus' ministry (before his D/B/R) then you didn't need to be re-baptized when Peter and the Apostles began preaching Jesus' baptism of Pentecost.

- When did the Apostles receive the indwelling of the Holy Spirit? They received the indwelling of the Holy Spirit after Jesus had arisen from the dead and gave it to them as He had promised (John 20:19-22). They were the first to receive the indwelling.

    o What was it that they received at Pentecost? At Pentecost (after Jesus had risen and appeared to them for 40 days and then ascended to heaven) the Lord empowered them with the "power" of the Holy Spirit. Acts 2:4 – Power, not indwelling; the demonstration of the power, tongues.

- What is the difference between "indwelling" of the Holy Spirit and "empowering" of the Holy Spirit?

    o Indwelling - is the fulfillment of the promise that when the Messiah came, God would be with everyone (Isaiah 44:3 and Acts 2:39).

- He is the means by which we are regenerated and resurrected (Romans 8:9-11).

  o Empowerment - is the special gift given to the Apostles and some early disciples enabling them to speak in tongues and do miracles in order to assist them in preaching the gospel and establishing the early church (Acts 2:4 and 8:4-6). Later on, this empowerment was transferred by the "laying on of the hands" of the Apostles (Acts 19:6).

- When did those who had been baptized by John (before Pentecost) receive the indwelling of the Holy Spirit?

  o They received the Indwelling of the Holy Spirit at Pentecost as Peter and the others began to preach and offer it to all. They had already prepared themselves for this day by repenting and being baptized according to John's command. Now forgiveness was available (through Jesus' sacrifice on the cross) and the Holy Spirit was given (because Jesus had returned to the Father) (John 15:26).

  o All those who had received John's baptism were granted forgiveness and the indwelling of the Holy Spirit at Pentecost. That was the promise. It was a delayed payment for those who had believed, repented and prepared ahead of time by receiving John's baptism.

  o All those who had not received John's baptism and heard the gospel on Pentecost were required to: believe in Jesus as the Son of God, repent of their sins, and be baptized in Jesus' name…and they too would receive the forgiveness and the indwelling of the Holy Spirit (Acts 2:38).

- What about the disciples in Acts 19:1-7, why were they re-baptized?

  - They were re-baptized because they received John's baptism after Pentecost. They were baptized to show that they were preparing for the kingdom to come.

  - Paul re-baptized them in the name of Jesus for forgiveness and the indwelling of the Holy Spirit. In this way they were baptized for the right reason and in the right way.

- Why does it seem that Apollos, their teacher, wasn't re-baptized but his students were?

  - Apollos received John's baptism during the time before Pentecost. He didn't need to be re-baptized, he needed to be taught more perfectly concerning the preaching of the gospel after Pentecost.

  - His students were baptized in John's baptism after Pentecost so they needed to be re-baptized.

- What does this mean for us today? People need to be re-baptized if:

1. They have been baptized the wrong way. In other words if they have been baptized by sprinkling or pouring and not by immersion.

2. They have been baptized for the wrong reasons. For example, some have been baptized in order to join a group or because it was their birthday. Many have done

it to please their parents or have been coerced by group pressure at camp.

However, the Bible explains that baptism is a response of faith in Jesus Christ as the Son of God and done for many reasons (to become a disciple – Matthew 28:18-19; to obey the gospel – Mark 16:15-16; to be born again – John 3:3-5; to be forgiven and receive the gift of the Holy Spirit – Acts 2:38; to be buried and resurrected with Christ – Romans 6:3-6; to clothe ourselves with Christ – Galatians 3:27; to appeal to God for a clear conscious – I Peter 3:21 etc.). These and many other passages in the Bible describe the many reasons one is baptized, and if one is immersed for any of these biblical reasons, they have done so according to God's will in His word.

However, if a person is baptized for a non–biblical reason such as doing so to please another or for an incorrect theological reason (like the 12 believers at Ephesus) then re-baptism is required.

In the same way that Paul made sure that these men had both the reason and method of baptism correct, we today should follow his inspired example when we carefully follow the Bible's teaching regarding the reason and manner that we are baptized. This is not "legalism" as some would charge, but a respectful and prudent attitude towards the teaching in the Scriptures concerning the reasons for and practice of baptism by modern day disciples of Jesus Christ.

- Is re-baptism common today? Yes, because so many people have been taught (sincerely but incorrectly) about the reasons and methods for baptism.

It's a question of love. Jesus said, "If you love Me, you will obey My word." John 14:15. Peter said, "We must obey God rather than men." Acts 5:29

Baptism is the believer's wedding ceremony with Christ. It is beautiful, acceptable and righteous if it is done exactly as the Lord has commanded it to be done. We, as mere humans, have no right to make changes to what God has ordained in His Word.

BibleTalk.tv is an Internet Mission Work.

We provide textual Bible teaching material on our website and mobile apps for free. We enable churches and individuals all over the world to have access to high quality Bible materials for personal growth, group study or for teaching in their classes.

The goal of this mission work is to spread the gospel to the greatest number of people using the latest technology available. For the first time in history it is becoming possible to preach the gospel to the entire world at once. BibleTalk.tv is an effort to preach the gospel to all nations every day until Jesus returns.

The Choctaw Church of Christ in Oklahoma City is the sponsoring congregation for this work and provides the oversight for the BibleTalk ministry team. If you would like information on how you can support this ministry, please go to the link provided below.

bibletalk.tv/support

Made in United States
Orlando, FL
19 March 2023